NATIVE PLANTS FOR CALIFORNIA GARDENS

Calycanthus occidentalis

FOR
CALIFORNIA GARDENS

LEE W. LENZ

RANCHO SANTA ANA BOTANIC GARDEN

CLAREMONT, CALIFORNIA

Printed in the United States of America
By Abbey Garden Press
132 West Union Street, Pasadena, California

FOREWORD

THIS BOOK is the outgrowth of a series of papers devoted to the botany and horticulture of California plants, published as the *Leaflets of Popular Information* by the Rancho Santa Ana Botanic Garden. An attempt has been made to select from the native flora those species which can be recommended as of value to gardeners, describing them in simple language and giving their cultural requirements as well as suggested uses in California landscaping and gardening. In order to make the identification of the plants easy for those not already familiar with them, the majority of the species are illustrated.

The gardener may well ask on what basis the choice of plants was made and he may look in vain for some particular one he considers to be of real garden value. Selection of the species, however, was made from the results of almost a quarter of a century of work in growing natives by the Rancho Santa Ana Botanic Garden and there is a special reason for the choice of each plant. Some groups, as for example the trees, are represented here by only a few species. The reason is that many of the trees are already so well known and so much has been written about them that it is considered unnecessary to treat them further.

In a number of groups such as the Penstemons where there are a great many very beautiful species which would appear to be most desirable garden subjects, only a few are discussed. The reason for this is that many are rather difficult to grow successfully and in such groups relative ease of growing must be carefully considered before recommending the plants to gardeners. In other cases, especially in the annuals, where ease of cultivation is general rather than exceptional, some described are already rather widely grown while others, though equally desirable, are little known and seldom seen.

In still other cases such as *Fremontia mexicana,* which admittedly is difficult for many to handle, the plants are recommended because of their exceptional beauty and it is believed that gardeners should attempt to provide the plants with the requirements necessary for their successful growth.

Because of the wide diversity in growing conditions to be found in California, some species can be recommended only for definite areas while others can be grown successfully in almost any part. Indeed it should be stressed that while the recommendations made here are primarily those for the southern part of the state, a great many of the plants can be grown equally well not only in other parts of California but also in many other parts of the Southwest.

While the California flora contains many plants of interest and importance to rock gardeners, succulent enthusiasts and others interested in special groups, no attempt has been made to include these in the present book.

Recently some of the more important groups of California ornamentals such as the Ceanothi, the Penstemons, and Diplacus have been treated in detail by authorities on the various groups and the reader is referred to the bibliography for references where this more detailed information may be obtained.

The author wishes to acknowledge his appreciation to Dr. Philip A. Munz, Director of the Rancho Santa Ana Botanic Garden, who first suggested the plan for the present book and who has so kindly checked the botanical descriptions and scientific names. Thanks is also due Mr. Percy C. Everett, Superintendent of the Botanic Garden, for much of the information on propagation and uses of the plants. The photographs unless otherwise noted were taken by M. and M. Carothers of La Jolla, California.

LEE W. LENZ

The kodachrome of *Calycanthus occidentalis* used on the frontispiece is by Brooking Tatum

DEDICATED TO THE MANY PLANT EXPLORERS

THROUGH WHOSE ZEAL AND DEVOTION THE

GRADENS OF THE WORLD HAVE BEEN

MADE BRIGHTER

TABLE OF CONTENTS

NATIVE PLANTS FOR CALIFORNIA GARDENS

INTRODUCTION

IT HAS BEEN only within recent years that Californians have begun to use native plants to any great extent about their homes, although it is known that at least a few of them were grown by gardeners in the early 1850's, and during the 1870's many of the natives were discussed in local horticultural publications where gardeners were urged to grow them. McMinn, in writing for the *Bulletin of the Garden Clubs of America* a few years ago, stated that among the reasons for the failure of gardeners to recognize the ornamental possibilities of California shrubs in the past was the inability of the public to secure them from plant nurseries, the hesitancy of the public in general to try out new plants, and the nearly complete absence of native plant promoters. To these reasons may be added the lack of understanding on the part of many gardeners of their cultural requirements. Today the picture has greatly changed and Californians are using more and more California plant material in landscaping their homes.

Within the past thirty years there have been established in southern California two botanical gardens devoted to the study and dissemination of information concerning native plants. At Santa Barbara the Santa Barbara Botanic Garden located in Mission Canyon applies itself entirely to the growing and demonstrating of horticultural possibilities of native California plants, while the Rancho Santa Ana Botanic Garden located at Claremont in Los Angeles County is devoted to both botanical and horticultural research in the field of California botany. Both of these institutions have gained wide experience in the growing and use of California plants; and through their publications, as well as visits to the botanical gardens themselves, the gardener may find answers to many of his questions. At the present time nearly all the larger nurseries handle the more common native California ornamentals and at least one nurseryman handles them exclusively.

I. BOTANICAL CHARACTERISTICS OF THE
CALIFORNIA FLORA

CALIFORNIA, extending as it does some eight-hundred miles in a north-south direction, and from the Pacific Ocean on the west to the slopes of the Great Basin and the Mojave and Colorado deserts in the east, and with altitudes of from 276 feet below sea-level in Death Valley to over 14,000 feet on Mt. Whitney, encompasses an area more diversified in topography and climate than is to be found in any other state. In this area has developed one of the most distinctive floras in North America.

The uniqueness of the California flora may be seen when it is realized what a large number of plants native to the state are to be found growing in no other area in the world. Of the few more than four thousand species listed in Jepson's *"Manual of the Flowering Plants of California"* over 1400 are found only in California. These plants, known as endemics, thus form more than one-third of the entire flora of the state. Some of the endemics such as the California Poppy, the Coast Live Oak and the Coast Redwood occur rather generally over large areas, in some instances even being found short distances outside of the state, while others may be restricted to a single locality. In the latter category may be mentioned the beautiful Santa Cruz Island Iron-wood *(Lyonothamnus floribundus* var. *asplenifolius)* known from only four of the Channel Islands, *Carpenteria californica* found only in a small area in the Sierra Nevada foothills, *Ceanothus impressus* from northwestern Santa Barbara County and *Iris munzii* which is found only in a few places in Tulare County.

The distinctive character of the flora of California, along with its high degree of endemism, sets the region apart from the rest of the United States as a separate botanical province comparable to such areas as the Cape of South Africa, Western Australia or portions of the Mediterranean.

With such a diversity of topographic features there is also an extreme range of climatic and soil conditions—all the way from the intense heat of the deserts during the summer to the permanent snowfields of the high Sierra Nevada. Thus the state has as great a range in temperature as is to be found anywhere in the North Temperate Zone. Variation in rainfall is equally striking. Some localities in northern California receive over one hundred inches of rain a year while areas in the desert may receive 2 to 3 inches of precipitatoin annually with occasional years when no rain is recorded.

One very important factor which strongly affects the plant life of much of the state is the seasonal distribution of the rainfall. This factor is of real importance to gardeners who may wish to use California ornamentals in their plantings. Most of the state has very definite wet and dry seasons and the native plants are highly adapted to this seasonal variation of precipitation. Rains usually begin in the late fall and occur sporadically throughout the winter with periods of light to heavy precipitation alternating with periods of sunny weather with no precipitation. Usually by the end of March the rainy season is about over and from then until the following fall, little or no moisture is received. Annual plants which are so abundant in the California flora usually germinate in the fall after the rains begin and continue to grow throughout the normally mild winter. These plants bloom during the spring and early summer after which they quickly ripen their seeds and by mid-summer many of them have entirely disappeared from the landscape. Much the same thing happens in the case of many native shrubs. Growth takes place during the winter and spring with the blooming period coming during the spring months after which the plants go into a rest period during the hot dry summer. It is this rest period during the summer

1

required by many of the plants that causes so much trouble to gardeners and the result has been that many of the finest California ornamentals have acquired a reputation of being difficult to grow.

When planted along with exotics which require frequent irrigation during the summer, natives may react differently to the water which they receive. Some of them appear at first to accept it and they will grow at a rapid rate for a time but after a season or so the plants suddenly die. This type of reaction is especially characteristic of many of the Ceanothi, Fremontias, etc. On the other hand, some of the shrubs from the northern part of the state, or from the Coast Ranges, react more favorably to summer watering and a number of them readily adapt themselves to ordinary garden culture. There are, however, exceptions and a few plants which, while found in nature in dry places, will grow well when given considerably more water than they are accustomed to having. Examples of this are the Sugarbush *(Rhus ovata)* and Nevin's Barberry *(Berberis nevinii)*, both native to well-drained dry hot areas in southern California and reported to do well in poorly-drained heavy adobe soil in the San Francisco Bay area.

Another factor affecting plant life is the soil which in California varies as widely as does the precipitation. Soil scientists have divided the state into three major provinces as far as soil texture is concerned. The first region is one of coarse-textured soils which are to be found in the Sierra Nevada, the deserts, and the major part of the state south of Los Angeles. The second province, consisting of clay loams, embraces much of the Coast Ranges and a large part of the northeast mountain area. The third province is assigned to the Great Valley, a very variable and complex province, but in some degree it reflects the soils of the surrounding higher elevations.

Besides soil texture there are two other factors which are important. One of them is the amount of humus in the soil and the other is the acidity or alkalinity of the soil. The average humus content of the surface soils is lowest in the desert regions and, except for tules and meadows, highest in the Coast Range valleys with the San Joaquin and Sacramento valleys intermediate between the two. The higher humus content in the Coast Range valleys is attributed to a greater humidity and a denser vegetation in that region.

As regards acidity or alkalinity it has been shown that while different soils vary widely, in general many of them in the drier and more desert regions tend to be strongly alkaline, while those found along the north coast may be often extremely acid. For the most part the agriculturally important soils tend to be nearly neutral and in no instance do they approach the extremes of alkalinity found in some of the desert areas or the acidity found along the Mendocino coast.

To summarize briefly, it may be said that the soils in the drier, hotter portions of the state tend to be coarse-textured, low in humus, and from nearly neutral to strongly alkaline. At the other extreme are the soils from the north coast area which tend to be fine-textured, high in humus, and from nearly neutral to strongly acid. The plants found in the different areas reflect these differences. Therefore the gardener living in southern California who wishes to grow plants native to the north coast may have to add humus to his soil as well as some material such as peat moss which will change the soil reaction from alkaline to acid if he is to succeed with these particular plants. Likewise, plants from dry areas such as the chaparral may, in the garden, require excellent drainage and a soil not too rich in humus for their best growth. Since most of the soil in southern California tends to be neutral to strongly alkaline the pH usually does not have to be taken into account except for "acid loving" plants such as the Western Azalea *(Rhododendron occidentale)*. Western Rhododendron *(Rhododendron macrophyllum)*, Salal *(Gaultheria shallon)* and *Lupinus polyphyllus* (one of the parents of the beautiful Russell hybrids).

In general it may be said that in order for the gardener to have the greatest success in growing native plants it will be necessary for him to understand something of the native habitat of the plants he is growing and the conditions under which they are found in nature. Once these are understood the essential requirements can then often be created rather easily in the garden.

2

In nature plants having similar habitat requirements will often be found growing together. Botanists have long studied these plant associations in an attempt to classify them and to determine the environmental factors which are responsible for their development. Drs. Philip A. Munz and David D. Keck after many years of study of the California flora have recognized twenty-eight plant communities which are grouped into eleven major vegetation types. In a recent paper[1] they have described the various climatic and soil conditions and have listed the plants which are indicators of these various communities. Since this information is of considerable interest to gardeners it will be briefly discussed here from the standpoint of the horticulturist.

The first of the major vegetation types which these authors describe is the Strand which in California is represented by the COASTAL STRAND plant community. This community includes the sandy beaches and dunes along the entire length of the state and is a region with an average rainfall of from 15-70 inches a year with much fog and wind. The plants found here are for the most part low or prostrate and from the horticultural standpoint the most important species are the Beach Strawberry *(Fragaria chiloensis)*, the Rose-colored Sand Verbena *(Abronia maritima)* and various species of *Mesembryanthemum*.

The next vegetation type includes two plant communities: the COASTAL SALT MARSH, and the FRESH WATER MARSH, neither of them of importance to the gardener.

The Scrub vegetation has been divided into six distinctive plant communities the first of which is the NORTHERN COASTAL SCRUB. This community occupies a narrow coastal strip extending from southern Oregon south to San Mateo County and from Pacific Grove to Point Sur. It is this plant community which occupies the area between the Coastal Strand described above and the Redwood Forest. The rainfall here is moderate to heavy averaging from 25-75 inches a year and the area is subjected to a great deal of fog and wind. This community contributes several plants of interest to gardeners including *Diplacus aurantiacus*, the Seaside Daisy *(Erigeron glaucus)*, the groundcover *Baccharis pilularis* var. *pilularis*, *Lonicera involucrata* var. *ledebourii*, *Ceanothus griseus* var. *horizontalis* and *C. thyrsiflorus* var. *repens*.

Farther south is the COASTAL SAGE SCRUB which occurs on dry rocky and gravelly slopes in the South Coast Ranges and from there south to Baja California. This area receives an average of from 10-20 inches of rainfall a year and experiences only an occasional frost. From this community comes a number of fine garden plants such as *Agave shawii*, *Berberis nevinii*, *Eriogonum giganteum*, *E. fasciculatum*, *Isomeris arborea*, *Leptodactylon californicum*, Lemonade Berry *(Rhus integrifolia)*, *Galvezia speciosa*, *Ribes malvaceum* var. *viridifolium*, *Lupinus longifolius*, *Nolina parryi*, *Penstemon antirrhinoides*, *Prunus ilicifolia*, *P. lyonii*, *Ribes speciosum*, *Romneya coulteri* and *Salvia leucophylla*.

The SAGEBRUSH SCRUB is found on the opposite side of the state where it occurs along the east base of the Sierra Nevada all the way from Modoc County south to the Laguna Mts. at altitudes of from 4000-7000 feet. It is characterized by having deep pervious soil and relatively low precipitation (8-15 inches), much of which comes in the winter as snow.

The next of the Scrub communities is the CREOSOTE BUSH SCRUB which is found on the slopes, fans and valleys in the deserts usually below 3500 feet and occurs from the southern end of Owens Valley south to Mexico. Here the rainfall is low, varying from 2-8 inches a year with some of it coming as summer showers. The soil is usually well-drained and the extremes of temperature are great. The plants found here include a number of cacti, *Atriplex hymenelytra*, *Beloperone californica*, *Fouquieria splendens*, *Isomeris arborea*, *Baileya multiradiata*, *Coreopsis calliopsidea*, and *Fallugia paradoxa*. The Desert Willow *(Chilopsis linearis)* occurs here along the water courses.

The ALKALI SINK community is found on poorly drained alkaline flats, playas, etc. and is of no importance as far as the gardener is concerned.

---

[1] Philip A. Munz and David D. Keck. California Plant Communities. El Aliso 2: 87-105, 1949. Supplement. ibid. 2: 199-202. 1950.

The next of the great vegetation types is the coniferous forest which Munz and Keck have divided into eight plant communities. Beginning in the north the first is the NORTH COASTAL CONIFEROUS FOREST which occurs along the outer North Coast Ranges from Mendocino County northward with restricted patches occurring as far south as Sonoma County. In altitude this community ranges from near sea-level to about 1000 feet. Rainfall is moderate to heavy averaging from 40-110 inches a year. The temperature is mild and equable and fogs are frequent. In this community are found many large ever-greens such as Arbor-Vitae *(Thuja plicata)*, Douglas Fir *(Pseudotsuga menziesii)*, and Lawson Cypress *(Chamaecyparis lawsoniana)*.

The CLOSED-CONE PINE FOREST is an interrupted forest extending from the Mendocino plains southward to Santa Barbara County and ranges in altitude from near sea-level to about 1200 feet. In the northern part of its range this community is found occupying rather barren soils on the seaward side of the redwood forest. Here the rainfall is from 20-60 inches a year and there is some fog. Among the plants growing in this com-munity are a number of interesting evergreens such as the Bishop Pine *(Pinus muricata)*, the Monterey Pine *(P. radiata)*, the Monterey Cypress *(Cupressus macrocarpa)* and the Gowen Cypress *(C. goveniana)*. Included among the shrubs are *Garrya elliptica, Lonicera involucrata* and a number of species of Ceanothus, *C. griseus* var. *horizontalis* probably being the most important one from the gardening standpoint. *Ribes sanguineum* var. *glu-tinosum* is also found here.

The REDWOOD FOREST community is well known to most people. It occupies the seaward side of the Coastal Ranges from Del Norte County in California south to San Luis Obispo County. In altitude it ranges from near sea-level to about 2000 feet. The rain-fall is moderate to heavy, ranging from 35-100 inches a year, and there is a great deal of fog even in the dry season. Besides the well-known *Sequoia sempervirens* this community contains a large number of interesting and beautiful species. Unfortunately many of them are difficult to handle in southern California where the environmental conditions are so very different from those to which the plants are accustomed. In addition to the Redwood and Douglas Fir other plants of interest include the Wax Myrtle *(Myrica californica)*, Salal *(Gaultheria shallon)*, *Rhododendron macrophyllum*, and the Sword Fern *(Polysti-chum munitum)*.

The DOUGLAS FIR FOREST is found in the North Coast Ranges from Mendocino County north with occasional scattered elements as far south as Sonoma and Marin coun-ties. For the most part the Douglas Fir Forest occupies the area east of the redwoods and in some places reaches an elevation of 4500 feet, while in other places it extends almost to the coast. The environmental conditions are much the same as they are in the Mixed Evergreen Forest. Besides the Douglas Fir other plants found here include the Tan Oak *(Lithocarpus densiflora)*, Madroño *(Arbutus menziesii)* and *Rhododendron macrophyllum*.

The YELLOW PINE FOREST is rather widespread in California, occurring in north-ern California at altitudes of 3000-6000 feet, in the Sierra Nevada at elevations of from 2000-6500 feet and in southern California at 5000-8000 feet. This community receives an average of from 25-80 inches of precipitation a year with part of it coming as snow. From this area come the Yellow Pine *(Pinus ponderosa)*, the Sugar Pine *(P. lambertiana)*, Incense Cedar *(Libocedrus decurrens)*, Douglas Fir *(Pseudotsuga menziesii)*, the Cali-fornia Black Oak *(Quercus kelloggii)*, *Ceanothus integerrimus*, the Thimble Berry *(Rubus parviflorus)*, the Mock Orange *(Philadelphus lewisii* var. *californica)*, Sequoiadendron *giganteum* and the California Nutmeg *(Torreya californica)*.

The RED FIR FOREST occurs above 6000 feet in the North Coast Ranges, from 5500-7500 feet in northern California, from 6000-9000 feet in the Sierra and from 8000-9500 feet in southern California. Here there is an average precipitation of from 35-65 inches a year with heavy winter snows and a short growing season of from 40-70 frost-free days. One of the most conspicuous trees found in this community is the Quaking Aspen *(Popu-lus tremuloides)*. From the standpoint of gardeners in the south this community is not of great importance nor is the LODGEPOLE FOREST which occurs in northeastern Cali-

4

fornia south to the central Sierra Nevada. Above this is the SUBALPINE FOREST which is the highest forest found in the state. This community is poorly represented in species of interest to gardeners in the warmer climates.

The next vegetation type recognized by Munz and Keck is the Mixed Evergreen Forest with only a single plant community, the MIXED EVERGREEN FOREST. This community is found along the inner edge of the Redwood Forest as well as on the higher hills within it and extends south as far as the Santa Cruz Mts., and the north side of the Santa Lucias at elevations of from 200-2500 feet. Here the rainfall is from 25-65 inches a year and there is some fog. This community contains a number of important ornamentals including such things as the Tan Oak *(Lithocarpus densiflora)*, Madroño *(Arbutus menziesii)*, Big-leaved Maple *(Acer macrophyllum)*, Mock Orange *(Philadelphus lewisii* var. *gordonianus)*, *Ceanothus thyrsiflorus, Rhododendron occidentale*, and the Mountain Dogwood *(Cornus nuttallii)*.

The Woodland-Savannah has been divided into the northern and southern Oak Woodlands and the Foothill Woodland plant communities. The NORTHERN OAK WOODLAND is found in the North Coast Ranges from Humboldt and Trinity counties south as far as Napa County and inland from the Redwood Forest to the Yolla Bolly Mts. where it occurs at altitudes of from 3000-5000 feet. Here there is an average of from 25-40 inches of precipitation a year with a growing season of from 6-9 months. As the name indicates, this community contains a number of oaks including *Quercus garryana*, the California Black Oak *(Q. kelloggii)* and the Canyon Oak *(Q. chrysolepis)*. The California Buckeye *(Aesculus californica)* also occurs here, as does *Ceanothus integerrimus*.

The SOUTHERN OAK WOODLAND is found in the inner valleys of southern California from Los Angeles County south to San Diego County. In some places in the San Jacinto Mts. it may ascend as high as 5000 feet. In this plant community the average rainfall may vary from 15-25 inches a year and there is a growing season of from 7-10 months. It is here that we find the familiar Coast Live Oak *(Q. agrifolia)*, Mesa Oak *(Q. engelmanii)*, Southern California Black Walnut *(Juglans californica)*, Sycamore *(Platanus racemosa)*, Forbes Cypress *(Cupressus forbesii)*, and two important shrubs, the Lemonade Berry *(Rhus integrifolia)* and the Sugarbush *(Rhus ovata)*.

The FOOTHILL WOODLAND community includes both the foothills and valley borders at altitudes of from 400-3000 feet, extending ocasionally as high as 5000 feet on warm slopes. This community occurs along the inner Coast Ranges from Trinity County south to Santa Barbara County and along the slopes of the Sierra Nevada foothills as far south as northwestern Los Angeles County. Here there are from 15-40 inches of rainfall a year with little or no fog and a growing season of from 6-10 months. The summers are hot and dry and the winter temperatures may be fairly low. A number of oaks are found here including the Coast Live Oak *(Q. agrifolia)* and the Valley Oak *(Q. lobata)* and in addition there are important ornamentals such as the Redbud *(Cercis occidentalis)*, Carpenteria californica, Fremontia californica, Rhamnus californica var. tomentella, the California Bay Tree *(Umbellularia californica)* and the interesting little Dutchman's Pipe vine, *Aristolochia californica. Iris munzii* also comes from this community.

Next is a plant community which is very well known to southern Californians and one which contains a greater number of shrubs of value to gardeners in this area than any other single community. This is the CHAPARRAL which is found on dry slopes and ridges in the Coast Ranges from Shasta County south, and below the Yellow Pine forest on the western slopes of the Sierra Nevada and the more southern mountains. Here the rainfall may average from 14-25 inches a year, the summers are hot and dry and the winters cool. The soils tend to be either rocky or gravelly or they may be fairly heavy. Here are found such plants as Chamise *(Adenostoma fasciculatum)*, Toyon *(Heteromeles arbutifolia)*, Coffee Berry *(Rhamnus californica)*, Red-berry *(R. crocea)*, *Yucca whipplei, Fremontia mexicana, F. californica, Acalypha californica, Clematis lasiantha, Lathyrus splendens, Ceanothus cyaneus, C. impressus, Garrya elliptica, Penstemon antirrhinoides, P. cordifolius, Salvia clevelandii*, and *Trichostema lanatum*.

5

The open grasslands of the state have been divided into two plant communities; the COASTAL PRAIRIE and the VALLEY GRASSLAND.

The COASTAL PRAIRIE is the open temperate hill-grasslands, glades or bald hills found on the western slopes of the outer and middle Coast Ranges from Mendocino and Trinity counties northward with scattered patches as far south as the San Francisco Bay area. The climate is similar to that found in the Northern Oak Woodland. This community consisted originally of bunch grass and numerous flowering herbs, but today it is partially superceded by annual introduced weedy grasses. From the gardener's standpoint the following plants are of interest: *Brodiaea pulchella, Iris douglasiana, Sisyrinchium bellum, Calochortus luteus* and *Ranunculus californica.*

The VALLEY GRASSLAND was originally found in the Great Central Valley and in the low hot valleys of the inner Coast Ranges but it occurs also along the coast from San Luis Obispo County south and in the Tehachapi Mts. as well as eastern San Diego County, where it ascends to about 4000 feet. This community is characterized by hot dry summers and cool rainy winters with an average rainfall of from 6-20 inches. It is this community, more than any other which is noted for its magnificent display of annuals following the wet seasons. Among the more conspicuous species are the California Poppy *(Eschscholzia californica),* annual lupines, Gilias, Orthocarpus, etc.

The ALPINE FELL-FIELDS are all above timberline on the highest mountains. While there are many most interesting plants found there, none of them is of importance to gardeners in the warmer areas.

The last vegetation type recognized by Munz and Keck is the Desert Woodland which they have separated into three plant communities: the NORTHERN JUNIPER WOODLAND, the PINYON-JUNIPER WOODLAND and the JOSHUA TREE WOODLAND.

The first of these includes the Great Basin Plateau which extends to the eastern base of the Sierra from Modoc County south to Mono County. Here the precipitation may average from 10-30 inches a year with much of it coming as snow and the growing season is from 2-5 months. Plants found here include *Juniperus occidentalis,* the Pinyon Pine *(Pinus monophylla)* and the common Great Basin Sagebrush *(Artemisia tridentata.)*

The PINYON-JUNIPER WOODLAND is also found along the east base of the Sierra Nevada in the White-Inyo ranges and from there south through the higher mountains of the Mojave Desert, where it occupies the area below the Yellow Pine Forest and above the Joshua Tree Woodland or Sagebrush Scrub. In this community rainfall averages 12-20 inches a year with some snow and some summer showers. Of interest to gardeners are *Fallugia paradoxa* and *Yucca schidigera.*

The JOSHUA TREE WOODLAND in California covers the well-drained mesas and slopes at elevations of from 2500-4000 feet or higher, from the southern end of the Owens Valley south to the Little San Bernardino Mts. The rainfall averages 6-15 inches a year with occasional summer showers and a growing season limited by moisture rather than by temperature. Here are found the familiar Joshua Tree *(Yucca brevifolia* and its variety *jaegeriana)* and *Juniperus californica.*

II. EARLY BOTANICAL
AND HORTICULTURAL COLLECTORS

AMONG the earliest Europeans to visit California were the Franciscans who arrived in 1769 at what is now San Diego, and it is there that they established their first mission. During the next few decades the Spanish Fathers introduced into California a great many European fruits and vegetables. This was only natural since in a country not especially noted for its abundance of native food-plants, it was necessary for them to produce food sufficient for themselves and their converts. Some idea of the wide variety of plants grown during the early days of the missions may be obtained from Vancouver's description of the gardens at Mission San Buenaventura where he landed in November, 1793.

"The garden at Buena Ventura far exceeded anything I had before met with in these regions, both in respect of the quantity, quality, and variety of its excellent productions, not only indigenous to the country, but appertaining to the temperate as well as torrid zone; not one species having yet been sown that had not flourished. These have princi-pally consisted of apples, pears, plumbs, figs, oranges, grapes, peaches, cocoa nut, sugar cane, indigo, and a great variety of the necessary and useful kitchen herbs, plants and roots. All these were flourishing in the greatest health and perfection, though separated from the sea-side only by two or three fields of corn; that were cultivated within a few yards of the surf."

Indeed it has been said that few of the familiar fruits of California remained to be intro-duced after 1800.

There is, however, no record that the Spanish Fathers sent any of the California plants back to Spain but they did occasionally record the occurrence of some of the more con-spicuous ones, as for example, the Coast Live Oak *(Quercus agrifolia)* which was first mentioned by Father Venégas in 1758 in his *"Natural and Civil History of California"* and there is some evidence that they used at least a few California natives for planting around their missions.

In general, the earliest expeditions to the New World were those whose primary pur-pose was that of conquest for gold or for new lands for the Royal Crowns. As interest developed in knowing what the new countries were like, later expeditions often included a staff of scientists who were to explore and collect the natural products of these foreign lands. In fact, it was not long before nearly all expeditions carried a working gardener, apart from the scientific staff, whose job it was to care for the live plants during the voyage home. One of the most famous of these sea-going gardeners was David Nelson who was on the ill-fated voyage of the *Bounty* under Captain Bligh when it was dispatched to Tahiti to collect plants of the Bread Fruit for introduction into the West Indies. Nelson was among those set adrift by the mutineers and he later died from exposure after reaching Timor. It is known that these men had special training for their job because the English botanist, Sir Joseph Banks in writing about Nelson said "He had been regularly educated at Kew as a gardener and learned there the art of taking care of plants at sea and guarding against the many accidents to which they are liable."

In 1785 the La Perouse Expedition sailed from France with two ships and seventeen scientists, among them the botanist Collignon who was destined to be the first man to botanize in California. It was during their stay at Monterey in September, 1786, that Collignon found and sent back to Europe seeds of an attractive herbaceous plant which was common along the beach, the Rose-colored Sand Verbena *(Abronia umbellata)*. According to some authorities this was the first California plant to be grown in the Old World. Collignon also collected a cone from one of the California conifers, probably the

Monterey Pine *(Pinus radiata)* which he sent to the *Jardin des Plantes* in Paris. The exact identity of the pine is uncertain because the trees long since have disappeared. It might be added that this expedition has the distinction of being the first to introduce the potato into California where it was planted at Monterey from material obtained earlier in Chile.

Between Collignon's visit in 1786 and the time when David Douglas, the greatest of all the California plant collectors, arrived in 1830 a number of other botanists visited California for brief periods of time and most of them collected at least a few of the more conspicuous plants which they saw.

Among these early collectors was Thaddeus Haenke, botanist and apothecary with the Spanish expedition under command of Alejandro Malaspina. In 1791, while at Monterey, Haenke obtained the brilliant flowered California Fuchsia, *(Zauschneria californica)* and Neé, another botanist with the same expedition later named and described two California oaks, the Coast Live Oak *(Quercus agrifolia)* and the Valley Oak *(Quercus lobata)* from specimens collected by officers from their ship.

The next botanist to reach the state was Archibald Menzies who in 1790 sailed with the Vancouver Expedition on a voyage which took him around the world. Menzies has the honor of being the first to find several of the now best known California plants, among them being the Redwood *(Sequoia sempervirens)*, the California Laurel *(Umbellularia californica)*, the Douglas Fir *(Pseudotsuga menziesii)* and the Madrone *(Arbutus menziesii)* which Pursh later named in honor of Menzies.

When the Russian expedition under command of Otto von Kotzebue visited San Francisco Bay for a short time in 1816, their botanist, Adelbert von Chamisso, and the ship's doctor, Johann Friedrich Eschscholtz, made a small collection of plants which included one of the state's most conspicuous flowers, the California Poppy *(Eschscholzia californica)*. Actually Chamisso and Eschscholtz were not the first to collect the plant since Menzies had found it earlier, but Menzies' specimen had not been studied or described at that time. It was left for still another botanist, David Douglas, to introduce the plant into cultivation a number of years later.

In November 1827, the Beechey Expedition reached California and Lay, the expedition's naturalist, and Collie, the surgeon, made a collection of plants from the San Francisco and Monterey areas. At least one species, the Fuchsia-flowered Gooseberry *(Ribes speciosum)* was introduced into cultivation from seed collected by Collie.

It is easy to criticize the early botanists for not making larger collections of plants or for not taking more seeds and living material back to Europe, but it must be remembered that these men often had other duties than just to botanize—as for example, Menzies and Eschscholtz were both doctors. Too, the ships which first sailed to the New World were small and undoubtedly space was at a premium. Anyone who has collected plants knows that they are bulky and that large numbers of them would require more space than would be available on board the ships of that day. In other instances the expeditions reached California during the seasons when there was not a great deal to collect, as in the case of the La Perouse Expedition which reached Monterey in September. La Perouse noted the unfavorableness of the season in his journal, writing "From the day of our arrival our botanists lost not a moment in augmenting their collections of plants but the season was not favorable; the heat of the summer had entirely dried everything, and the seeds were scattered upon the earth."

In at least one instance the commander of the expedition failed to cooperate in the matter of taking living plants back to Europe. Menzies had a glass Wardian case on the quarter-deck for living material but Vancouver assigned other duties to the man who was supposed to care for them and when Menzies complained that he had lost many of his best plants through this action, Vancouver placed him under arrest for "insolence and contempt." Even today with all the facilities of high-speed transportation and modern handling methods many attempts at plant introduction fail.

In the early part of the 19th Century the Russians visited the Pacific Coast in search of sea-otter and fur seal and in 1812, a short distance north of Bodega Bay, they established Fort Ross which they occupied until it was bought by Sutter in 1841. During this period

8

seeds and specimens of a number of the plants found in that area were sent to St. Petersburg. Not a great deal is known about the Russian collectors except that one of them was I. G. Vosnesensky. The St. Petersburg Imperial Botanic Garden Seed Lists for the years 1834-1844 give a number of California species which were described from specimens grown from seed, many of which were collected in the vicinity of Bodega Bay and the Russian River.

We next come to the greatest of all the early plant explorers and collectors, a young Scotchman, David Douglas, in whose honor one of the grandest of all our evergreens, the Douglas Fir, is named.

While Menzies, Chamisso, and Eschscholtz had collected many of the more common and conspicuous plants, it was Douglas who was the first botanist to travel and collect extensively in the state. Not only did he make botanical specimens, but most important of all from the standpoint of the horticulturist, he gathered seeds of a great many species which he later sent to England where they were grown in gardens for the first time. Many Douglas introductions became extremely popular and were common in gardens in Europe within a matter of a few years. It may truthfully be said that through the work of David Douglas the horticultural world was first made conscious of the vast storehouse of ornamentals which were to be found in California.

In England, after the close of the Napoleonic Wars, there was an increased interest in horticulture and a great demand developed for new and unusual plants. It is, therefore, not surprising that during the next few decades great numbers of ornamentals were introduced into cultivation from all parts of the world.

In 1804, an organization known as the Horticultural Society of London (later the Royal Horticultural Society) was founded, its general purpose being "to encourage and elevate the study and practise of horticulture." By 1823 this organization had about fifteen-hundred members and it was this group that sent Douglas to collect in the New World.

In 1823, Douglas left England for the New World where he landed at New York City in early August. The primary object of this first visit was "to investigate the latest developments in fruit-growing and to obtain specimens of new trees, as well as to collect any interesting plants or seeds he found." When he returned to England he took with him one plant native to the West Coast, the Oregon Grape *(Berberis aquifolium)* which he had obtained from a nursery in New York. It had been introduced there from seed collected by Lewis and Clark on their famous expedition to the Pacific Northwest in 1804-06.

The following year Douglas was sent again to the New World but to the West Coast on this trip. No stop was made in California and the ship anchored in the Columbia River in April of 1825. From that time until 1827, he worked in what are now the states of Oregon and Washington. So successful was his collecting there that he set a record for introducing into England more plants than ever before had been introduced by any individual from any country.

Six months after his return to London he was again anxious to start on another expedition but this time to the area farther south—to California. He was told that at that time the Indians were so unfriendly that the Society did not want to send him. That, however, was not the real reason. The Horticultural Society had decided not to sponsor any more collecting expeditions because they believed that "extensive correspondence with every accessible country now renders such a means of procuring horticultural novelties less important than it has been heretofore."

However, by July 1829, the Society had changed its policy and had decided to send Douglas to western North America after all, this time to explore the botanical treasures of the interior of California and to make them known as he had those of the Columbia River area. This was good news for Douglas and in October, 1829, he again sailed for the New World. After rounding Cape Horn the ship called at Honolulu and then sailed for the West Coast and in early June of 1830 he was again at the Columbia. After spending the summer in the Pacific Northwest, Douglas left Fort Vancouver and arrived at Monterey shortly before Christmas. From that time until 1832 he remained in California. To list the plants he collected during those years would require many pages. There is one very unfortunate thing about Douglas's California collections and that is the loss of the journal describing his travels in the state in an accident on the Fraser River, making it often difficult to know the exact locality where he collected many of his specimens. During the summer of 1832 he left Monterey and sailed for Honolulu.

Two years later while exploring the slopes of Mauna Kea on the island of Hawaii, Douglas fell into a pit dug for capturing wild cattle and was killed by an enraged animal. Thus ended the career of the man who more than anyone else brought the wonders of the California flora to the attention of the world.

Up to now we have considered all botanical collectors regardless of whether they gathered seeds and living plants or not. After the time of Douglas, increasing numbers of botanists and horticultural collectors visited California, some of them from Europe; but more important, botanists began to arrive from the eastern part of the United States, either alone or with the early exploring parties which were sent west. In the ensuing years an ever increasing interest was shown in the flora of California with large numbers of plants being collected from all parts of the state. Such names as Thomas Coulter, Thomas Nuttall, W. H. Brewer, H. N. Bolander, C. C. Parry, and Albert Kellogg, among others, stand out conspicuously in the botanical history of the state. In 1876 there appeared the first volume of the *"Botany of the California Geological Survey"* prepared by Sereno Watson of Harvard University from plants collected by various field botanists attached to the survey. In 1880 the second volume of this pioneer work was published.

Since our primary interest is in the men who brought California plants to the attention of gardeners and horticulturists, we will consider here only those who, besides preparing dried specimens, also collected living material.

In 1845 the Horticultural Society of London again decided to send a man to California and in the Gardeners' Chronicle for March 8 of that year a notice appeared saying that "the beautiful vegetation of California is still but little known in our gardens. Mr. Douglas's discoveries, interesting as they were, are only an indication of what might still be done, and his collections arrived in bad condition." The man chosen this time to go to California on behalf of the Society was Theodor Hartweg. Hartweg, a young German gardener, had come to England some years before and the Horticultural Society had already sent him on one expedition, that time to Mexico to collect seeds and plants for them. He had spent seven years in Mexico and had sent back to the Society many seeds and plants as well as botanical specimens. In 1846 Hartweg arrived at Monterey and before the end of the year had dispatched a package of seeds and bulbs to England. These, however, were lost when the Mexican vessel on which they were travelling was captured by the Americans. During the autumn of that year he collected more seeds and a small number of these were later received by the Society. One of the plants which the Society was especially anxious to obtain was the California Fuchsia *(Zauschneria californica)* about which they wrote, "We trust it will not disappoint the expectations that have been formed on it." That they were not disappointed when the plants bloomed may be seen in the remarks made by the English botanist, Lindley, concerning the plant. "This curious plant" he wrote "which it has long been an object to obtain proves to be a species of much horticultural interest."

In 1847, Hartweg left Monterey for the foothills of the Sierra Nevada and he has the distinction of being the first botanist to collect in the Sierra. He later collected in the Salinas Valley and on that trip went as far south as San Luis Obispo. In 1848 he sailed for Europe with his materials. It is not known exactly how many plants were introduced into cultivation from seed he took, however, it is known that over eighty-five new species were described from his collections. It is said that the Society was not altogether satisfied with the results of his work in California and they blamed him especially for not securing seed of the Santa Lucia Fir *(Abies bracteata)*. He had, however, attempted to obtain seed and in his journal wrote that he had cut down a number of trees but found only immature cones, and those frozen.

By that time plants from the Pacific Coast had become so popular in Europe that the

10

renowned nursery firm of James Veitch and Sons of Exeter, England, sent a man to America to collect for them. The man selected was William Lobb who arrived in San Francisco in 1849. The Veitches were especially interested in having Lobb obtain seeds of certain trees discovered earlier by Menzies, Coulter, Douglas, and others, a number of which had not yet been introduced into cultivation. Without a doubt the most remarkable introduction made by Lobb was that of the Big Tree *(Sequoiadendron giganteum)*. Dr. Albert Kellogg had shown him specimens of the Big Tree collected from the Calaveras Grove by a Mr. Hutchins who lived in the area. Upon seeing the specimens Lobb became so enthusiastic that he left immediately for the Sierra where he dug two living trees which he carried to England on the first steamer leaving San Francisco. Lobb returned to California in the autumn of 1854 and continued to work for the Veitch nursery until 1857. After he left their employment he remained in California where he carried on his seed collecting until his death in 1863. Among the shrubs introduced into cultivation by Lobb are a number of species of Ceanothus such as *Ceanothus papillosus, C. veitchianus,* and *C. velutinus.* Lobb also re-introduced *Fremontia californica,* one plant of which had been grown in England before from seed sent by a Mr. Wrench.

At about this time there was another botanical collector working in the state, a man by the name of John Jeffrey. He had arrived on the Pacific Coast in 1851 on behalf of the Scottish-Oregon Expedition, an association formed in Edinburgh for the exploitation of the natural products of Western North America. The money for the expedition had been raised by subscription and subscribing members were each to receive a portion of the material collected. Little is known about Jeffrey's collecting except that he was in California in 1852. It seems that at first he did very well but later tired of the work and after joining an expedition which was to explore the Colorado and Gila Rivers in Arizona he was never heard from again. It is, however, known that Jeffrey collected over five hundred species, seeds of a number of which were sent to Edinburgh. Listed among his introductions are *Pinus balfouriana* and *Pinus jeffreyi.*

Another early collector about whom little is known is Thomas Bridges, who, after spending a number of years collecting in South America, came to California in 1858. It is definitely known that Bridges collected in Mariposa County, in the "Scott and Trinity Mts. near Yreka" and in the Coast Ranges of Santa Clara County. W. H. Brewer, a botanist from Yale University, mentions meeting Bridges in 1863 and says that he "has been supplying the gardens of England and Scotland with seeds, and the herbariums with plants from this coast for the last few years." The most famous plant that is connected with Bridges's name is not a California species but rather the giant Amazonian water-lily, *Victoria regia.* This most extraordinary plant producing leaves as much as six feet in diameter was introduced into cultivation from seeds collected by Bridges in 1845 near the headwaters of the Amazon. In the California flora his name is to be remembered by one of the Penstemons, *P. bridgesii.*

A number of California lilies, among them *Lilium humboldtii, L. washingtonianum,* and *L. pardalinum,* were first collected by Benito Roezl who was in California in 1869. Not a great deal is known about him except that he apparently took huge quantities of plants which were then sent to Europe. In one instance it is reported that he made a shipment containing ten tons of material. It is also reported that he went from San Francisco to San Diego to collect *Delphinium cardinale* of which he obtained some two thousand plants. Unfortunately when the plants bloomed they turned out to be a blue-flowered species instead of the red-flowered *cardinale.*

Still another period of increased interest in California plants came in the 1890's when the English gardeners started a reaction against the stiffness and formality charactersitic of their gardens during the period of "carpet-bedding" and "color massing." It was then that the herbaceous border and the rock garden began to come into their own. This new trend in gardening brought with it a number of problems for the nurseryman. No longer was it sufficient for him merely to obtain new colors or variations in size and form of the familiar garden plants but he had to look for new species which would fit the requirements of this new trend. Thus nurserymen began looking for species which had never been in cultivation or which had been introduced earlier and lost. Since they were searching for plants to be grown in the open in England, these would have to come from a temperate zone, or, if from warmer areas, from the higher altitudes where it was cooler. One such area was the west coast of North America and again California was turned to to supply new plants for gardens. Earlier in the century gardeners had been willing to pay more for plant oddities and it had been possible for them to send men to the desired regions to collect for them. Thus Douglas and Hartweg both had been sent to the Pacific Coast by the Horticultural Society of London. This method of obtaining new plants was no longer possible and the nurserymen had to depend upon local collectors and resident dealers for new plants.

One of these men was Carl Purdy of Ukiah. By 1881 Purdy had already done some collecting of bulbs and seeds for the director of Central Park in New York City and it was that year that he decided that collecting might be a good profession to follow and he wrote the well-known firm of Wallace and Sons in England telling them of his plans. Wallace was most enthusiastic over the possibilities of California bulbs in England and entered into an agreement with Purdy to have bulbs shipped to them. However, the first shipment, a large one, was ruined when the ship arrived three months late and the firm cancelled their agreement.

In 1887, John Lewis Childs of New York ordered five thousand Calochortus bulbs from Purdy to be used as premiums for subscriptions to a small magazine he was then publishing. The following year he ordered twenty-five thousand bulbs and in 1889, seventy-five thousand. During that year alone Purdy distributed over a quarter of a million bulbs—all of them collected from the wild. The panic of 1892 cut off most of the American business but that same year Wallace, having reorganized his firm, again ordered bulbs from Purdy. These later shipments arrived in good condition and soon he was importing huge quantities of California bulbs into England. Among them were Brodiaeas, Camassias, Erythroniums, Lilies, and many species of Calochortus, including the very beautiful, but difficult, *Calochortus kennedyi* from the desert. For the next few years great interest was shown in the bulbous plants from the West Coast, especially Calochortus, and some English catalogues listed as many as twenty or more species, nearly all of them bulbs imported from California. However, the Calochorti, many of them coming as they do from hot areas did not respond well to the cool damp climate of England and consequently soon lost their popularity. Today they are considered, along with the Oncocyclus irises, as very desirable but for the most part difficult garden subjects.

Another horticulturist whose name is connected with the introduction of two very desirable California plants is Miss Kate Sessions of San Diego. Born in San Francisco, Miss Sessions moved to San Diego in 1883 where she soon established a place for herself in horticultural circles of that city. Although not a specialist in native plants she recognized the horticultural importance of the now popular and well-known San Diego Lilac *(Ceanothus cyaneus)* and *Fremontia mexicana,* and it was largely through her efforts that these shrubs, both native to San Diego County, were introduced into cultivation.

Finally we come to a man who has done more to popularize the use of native plants in California than anyone else. Theodore Payne, born in England, came to Los Angeles in 1893. From the time of his arrival in California Payne took a keen interest in native plants, with many of which he was already familiar, having seen them growing in gardens of his native England. At an early date Payne viewed with alarm the rapid destruction of many of our finest species from ruthless picking, from the advance of agriculture which caused thousands of acres of wild flowers to be plowed under, from excessive and uncontrolled grazing, and from commercial collectors who stripped large areas of plants for market.

In 1903 Payne decided to start his own nursery and one of the first things he did was to collect seeds of a variety of native California plants which he grew and offered for sale. About 1906 Payne issued the first catalogue devoted entirely to California wild flowers. A modest publication with the picture of the California Poppy on the front cover, it listed fifty species recommended for California gardens. Since that time he has never ceased his campaign for the use of more and more native plants in California.

III. THE USES OF NATIVE PLANTS

IN ORDER for a gardener to grow successfully and to enjoy California plants, it is essential that he give considerable thought not only to their cultural requirements but also to their placement within the garden. Perhaps the ideal way to handle many of them is to grow natives in areas by themselves rather than to try to intersperse them in plantings with exotics. There are a number of reasons why this may be desirable; one being that many of the natives require a type of handling that is quite different from that of the commonly grown ornamentals. This is especially true in the matter of the water requirements of the plants and, as pointed out in an earlier chapter, some California natives cannot tolerate excessive moisture during the summer months. The reason for this is that much of California enjoys what is known as a Mediterranean type climate, i.e. warm dry summers and cool to mild wet winters, and many of the natives have become highly adapted to this cycle. Besides the Mediterranean, this type of climate is found in the Cape Region of South Africa and parts of Australia. Many of the unusual and very beautiful ornamentals growing in these areas either require, or at least tolerate, the same treatment as do our natives. Therefore it is possible to combine California plants with those from other areas having the same cultural requirements. Plantings of this type can be most effective and their true value will be realized more and more as water becomes an increasing problem in southern California. Even at the present time one of the most frequent questions asked about a new plant is: how much water will it require?

Another factor to be considered, though not of as great importance, is that some of our finest ornamentals go through a short period during late summer and early fall when they are nearly leafless. The beautiful Fuchsia-flowered Gooseberry *(Ribes speciosum)* is a good example of such a plant. It is during this period that some people may object to the appearance of the plants, especially if they are placed where they would be conspicuous during that time. To be sure, not all natives have an untidy period and a great many of them are beautiful during the entire year, as for example the Toyon, which in addition to its handsome evergreen leaves, is covered in early summer with large clusters of white flowers and these are then followed in late fall and winter by masss of red berries.

For those who do not wish to use California plants exclusively, or in the case of small gardens, there still may be areas where even the most difficult natives can be grown successfully. Often there is a corner, bank or other spot where it is not easy to grow things, either because it is hard to water or the soil is rocky and poor. With careful planning these areas can often be turned into interesting native gardens where even the most exacting of the California plants will thrive.

California ornamentals are also admirably suited for landscaping vacation homes whether at the beach, in the mountains or on the desert. The reason for their usefulness here is that after becoming established the plants will continue to grow and flourish with considerably less care than would be required by the majority of the exotics.

While the experienced gardener often has no need to consult special planting lists, it is believed that they are of value especially for beginners and those who may not be familiar with certain of the less common of the native ornamentals. For that reason the following groupings have been prepared.

ANNUAL BEDDING PLANTS

Among the plants enumerated here are some which by nature are perennials but are included because they are best treated as annuals.

Abronia villosa
Baeria maritima
Baileya multiradiata
Chorizanthe staticoides
Clarkia elegans
Coreopsis bigelovii
Coreopsis calliopsidea
Eschscholzia species
Gilia species

Godetia species
Layia platyglossa var. *elegans*
Linanthus grandiflorus
Lupinus nanus
Mentzelia lindleyi
Nemophila species
Oenothera deltoides var. *cognata*
Phacelia viscida

PERENNIAL BEDDING PLANTS

Aquilegia eximia
Coreopsis maritima
Diplacus species and hybrids
Erigeron glaucus
Eriogonum grande var. *rubescens*
Eriophyllum lanatum var. *arachnoideum*
Heuchera maxima

Iris douglasiana and hybrids
Lobelia cardinalis var. *splendens*
Mimulus cardinalis
Penstemon species
Sisyrinchium bellum
Zauschneria californica

PERENNIAL PLANTS FOR SEMI-SHADE

Aquilegia eximia
Asarum caudatum
Fragaria californica
Heuchera maxima

Iris douglasiana
Lobelia cardinalis var. *splendens*
Mimulus cardinalis

GROUND COVERS

Asarum caudatum
Baccharis pilularis var. *pilularis*
Fragaria californica

Fragaria chiloensis
Micromeria chamissonis

EVERGREEN HEDGES

Acalypha californica
Myrica californica
Prunus lyonii

Rhus integrifolia
Rhus ovata
Rhamnus crocea
Prunus ilicifolia

SHRUBS, DECUMBENT TO ERECT

Leptodactylon californicum

Ribes viburnifolium

SHRUBS; LOW TO MEDIUM HEIGHT, EVERGREEN

FILLERS AND FOUNDATION PLANTING

Acalypha californica
Atriplex hymenolytra
Berberis aquifolium
Berberis nevinii
Carpenteria californica

Fallugia paradoxa
Galvezia speciosa
Rhamnus crocea var. *typica*
Rhus integrifolia
Trichostema lanatum

14

SHRUBS; TALL FILLERS, BACKGROUND AND SCREEN PLANTING

Adenostoma sparsifolium
Arctostaphylos insularis
Ceanothus species and hybrids
Cercocarpus traskiae
Cercis occidentalis
Comarostaphylis diversifolia
Heteromeles arbutifolia

Myrica californica
Prunus ilicifolia
Prunus lyonii
Rhus laurina
Rhus ovata
Garrya elliptica

DECIDUOUS SHRUBS FOR SEMI-SHADE

Calycanthus occidentalis
Lonicera involucrata

Ribes aureum
Styrax occidentalis var. californica

EVERGREEN, OR SEMI-EVERGREEN SHRUBS FOR PARTIAL SHADE

Berberis aquifolium
Carpenteria californica
Myrica californica
Penstemon cordifolius

Ribes sanguineum
Ribes speciosum
Ribes viburnifolium

ACCENT SHRUBS

Agave shawii
Berberis nevinii
Ceanothus species and hybrids
Cercis occidentalis
Chilopsis linearis
Comarostaphylis diversifolia
Dendromecon rigida var. rhamnoides
Eriogonum giganteum
Fouquieria splendens
Fremontia californica
Fremontia mexicana

Heteromeles arbutifolia
Lupinus longifolius
Myrica californica
Nolina parryi
Penstemon antirrhinoides
Penstemon cordifolius
Ribes sanguineum
Ribes speciosum
Romneya coulteri
Yucca schidigera
Yucca whipplei

SHRUBS WITH ATTRACTIVE FRUITS

Berberis aquifolium
Berberis nevinii
Comarostaphylis diversifolia
Heteromeles arbutifolia

Lonicera involucrata
Myrica californica
Rhamnus crocea
Ribes aureum

SHRUBS TOLERATING SOME SUMMER WATER

Arctostaphylos insularis
Berberis nevinii
Calycanthus occidentalis
Cercis occidentalis
Cercocarpus traskiae
Chilopsis linearis

Heteromeles arbutifolia
Lonicera involucrata
Myrica californica
Rhus ovata
Ribes aureum

SHRUBS RECOMMENDED ONLY FOR NEARLY FROST-FREE AREAS

Acalypha californica

Rhus laurina

VINES

Aristolochia californica
Clematis lasiantha

Lathyrus splendens
Vitis girdiana

IV. THE PROPAGATION AND HANDLING
OF NATIVE PLANTS

IN GENERAL California annuals are easy to handle and the seeds can be sown any time from late fall to early spring in the open ground where the plants are to flower; and many of them, if left undisturbed, will re-seed themselves and appear year after year without further attention. Indeed many of the perennials may also be treated in the same manner. However, since many gardeners will not want the same species in the same location every year, they will find it best to sow the seed annually where they want the plants to bloom.

In the case of the trees and shrubs, as well as a number of perennials, it is better to start the seeds either in flats or prepared seedbeds and later move them to the locations in which they are to be grown.

Equipment

For starting seeds ordinary greenhouse flats are probably the most satisfactory pieces of equipment available. These may be purchased ready-made or can be constructed at home from scrap material. Flats vary in size; however one 18 inches square and about 2½ inches deep is usually considered as standard. At the Rancho Santa Ana Botanic Garden two sizes have been used, the standard 18 by 18 inches and a half flat 9 by 18 inches. The smaller size is useful when small quantities of seed are available, or when only a few plants are needed. If still smaller areas are needed dividers can be used. Shallow round 6-inch clay seed pans are also useful and are used at the Botanic Garden at the present time for small lots of seeds.

In many cases it is necessary to transplant seedlings from the flats to individual containers before they are finally moved to the garden. For this purpose ordinary 2-inch clay pots are recommended. There are, however, a number of other products available such as square, bottomless bands of thin wood or heavy tar-paper, which fit together in the seed flats. The tall ones are especially useful for plants with long taproots. For seedlings which are difficult to handle the clay pots are probably better than the bands since the roots are disturbed less when they are removed for planting.

In the case of shrubs and trees which are to be held over the first season, gallon cans are recommended since the plants will require less watering than if they are grown in clay pots. Another reason making gallon cans more desirable is that the roots quickly grow through the hole in the bottom of the pots.

Recently there has appeared on the market a crimped, tapered, metal pot of approximately the same size as the gallon can. While the original cost of these containers is slightly higher than gallon cans, they can be used over again, an important consideration for the gardener.

If trees or shrubs are to be held over for more than a year in most cases they should be transplanted from gallon to five-gallon cans.

While a greenhouse and lath house are essential pieces of equipment for the propagation of large numbers of plants, the average gardener who wishes to grow only enough plants for his own use can usually do so very easily in his backyard without the necessity of putting out large sums of money for equipment. If a lath house is not available, plants grown in pots or gallon cans can be placed in filtered shade under trees, or a temporary shade may be made by building a framework and covering it with a light material such as cheesecloth or some of the surplus camouflage materials which have appeared on the market in recent years. These temporary shades can then be removed during the winter months and the plants allowed to receive full sun during a portion of the year.

For the propagation of plants by cuttings, some sort of a propagating frame is necessary. While many types can be used, the simplest form is merely a wooden box with a few holes in the bottom and a piece of glass over the top. The frame is then partially filled with a rooting mixture into which the cuttings are placed. While this simple structure is sufficient for some of the more easily rooted cuttings, a more elaborate structure is needed for the more difficult species. The construction of propagating frames and the various rooting mixtures will be fully discussed under asexual propagation. If only a few cuttings are to be rooted an ordinary bell-jar or wide-mouthed gallon bottle is most useful.

Seed Germination

A seed has been defined as "a young plant packed and ready for transport to wherever it may be wanted to start growing." More exactly it may be said that a seed contains a young embryo together with a supply of food sufficient to establish the plant in a new location and the whole enclosed in a protective structure called the seed-coat. Germination then is the resumption of growth by the embryo when given proper conditions of heat, moisture, and air.

While the seeds of most plants germinate readily without treatment of any kind, others may be very difficult or slow. This is especially true of those of a number of California natives.

Among the reasons for slow germination is that the seeds may possess a very hard seed-coat which is impervious to both air and water. When this is the case germination may be hastened in several ways; the oldest and best known being scarification. This simply means scratching or cutting the seed-coat. In the case of large seeds such as those of lupine or Cercis a knife may be used to nick the seed-coat, or it can be punctured with a needle. Smaller seeds may be rubbed between or over pieces of sandpaper. Another method which has been found to be very useful is soaking seeds in hot water before planting. For Ceanothi the water should be heated to 180-200°F. and the seeds placed in it and allowed to remain in the cooling water for 24 hours before they are planted. Some seeds such as those of *Ceanothus sorediatus* are apparently not even injured by boiling for a short time. Several years ago Lammerts reported excellent germination with Ceanothus seed that had accidentally been allowed to soak in water for five days following the hot water treatment.

Other species which respond well to the hot water treatment are *Rhus integrifolia, R. ovata,* and *Cercis occidentalis.*

Another method which has been successful in germinating some plants is to treat the seed with acid for a short time. For this purpose it is placed in a glass jar and concentrated sulphuric acid (obtainable at drug and hardware stores) is then added. The volume of the acid should be about twice that occupied by the seeds and the mixture should be stirred occasionally. The length of time required for the treatment varies. For *Rhus integrifolia* Mirov and Kraebel recommend 4 hours or more, depending on the age of the seeds, while *R. trilobata* was found to germinate best after a 3-hour treatment. At the Rancho Santa Ana Botanic Garden it has been found that *Lupinus succulentus* seed germinated well after an 8 hour treatment. It should be pointed out that sulphuric acid can be very dangerous to use unless care is taken in its handling. After the seeds have been treated, the acid should be carefully poured off and saved and the seeds then thoroughly washed with a large amount of water. Great care should be used in adding water to the seeds after removing the acid. Mirov and Kraebel recommend using a quart jar of the kind employed for home canning. After the acid is removed a perforated lid is placed over the jar in the center of which there is a piece of glass, or copper tubing, which reaches to the bottom of the jar. One end of a piece of rubber tubing is then attached to the end of the tube while

17

the other end is attached to the water faucet. After the seeds have been thoroughly washed they should be planted immediately.

In place of the acid a strong lye solution can also be used. For *Garrya elliptica* McMinn recommends treating the seeds for 24 hours and then stratifying them for three months. However, this may not always be necessary since at the Botanic Garden *G. elliptica* has germinated in less than three months with no treatment of any kind. As in the case of the acid, great care should be exercised in handling the lye solution.

Dormancy of hard-coated seeds may also be overcome by planting them in soil which is subjected to alternate freezing and thawing during the winter. However, this method is of little value in warm climates unless the freezing compartment of a refrigerator is made to substitute for the low temperatures which much of the country experiences during the winter months.

Another major factor influencing seed germination in a number of plants is a process called "after-ripening." One form of after-ripening requires a combination of moisture, low temperature, and time. Since the correct combination of these three factors may not occur every year in nature, seeds may lie in the ground for years. However, for practical purposes it has been found that this type of dormancy may be broken by a process called "stratification." This consists essentially of planting the seed in flats or small containers in moist sand or peat moss, or a combination of the two, and placing the container in a refrigerator or in a cool place, such as a cellar, for varying lengths of time, usually 2-3 months. Among the species which have responded well to stratification at the Rancho Santa Ana Botanic Garden have been *Cornus nuttallii,* certain high altitude penstemons, lilies, roses, *Prunus virginica* var. *demissa* and many others. In the case of *Cornus nuttallii* untreated seeds germinated slowly over a long period of time whereas the stratified seeds germinated very evenly so that all the seedlings were ready to transplant at the same time. Recently Roof[1] has shown that if the fruits of *Cornus nuttallii* are gathered in September or October and the pulp cleaned from the nutlets and the fresh seed sown immediately germination will take place during the fall and the young seedlings can then be potted in late winter while they are still dormant. A similar situation exists in strawberries where if the seed is sown as soon as the fruit is ripe without allowing the seed opportunity to dry, almost every seed will start growing within a few days; whereas if the planting is delayed a few weeks and the seed dries, germination will not occur for months.

Another important factor influencing seed germination and one about which little is known in the case of most native plants is temperature, since few controlled experiments have been made. It has been reported that Apache Plume *(Fallugia paradoxa)* germinates best at 60-70°F. At the Rancho Santa Ana Botanic Garden the best results have been obtained when the seeds of this species were planted in September, a time when temperatures might well be within these limits.

Some very interesting work on the desert annuals has been reported by Barton of the Boyce Thompson Institute for Plant Research. She found that seeds of some species may fail to grow when fresh, or, if they do, they may require comparatively low temperatures or a combination of low and high temperatures. However, with aging of the seed there is a widening in the temperature range at which growth can take place. From the point of view of continuance of the species in nature this delay might be of great value to the plant. By requiring a specific temperature or combination of temperatures for germination of fresh seed, young plants would not be produced at a time unfavorable for their survival. Similarly, the low temperature requirements together with a degree of dormancy of the fresh seeds of winter annuals, would prevent their germination following the first summer rains since these rains are usually accompanied by high temperatures which would kill the seedlings. By the time the more favorable winter rains arrive the range of temperature required would have broadened somewhat and the dormancy disappeared by dry storage so that germination would occur.

---

[1] James Roof. *Growing California's Five Dogwoods.* Jour. Calif. Hort. Soc. 12: 51-58, 1951.

A rather unusual method has been discovered which facilitates germination in a number of important native ornamentals such as Romneya, Dendromecon, Juniperus, and Dicentra. The seeds are sown in flats or pots and covered lightly with soil after which a layer of dry pine needles or straw is placed over the flat and set afire. After the material has burned the flats are watered. The idea for this method occurred from observing how some plants appear in large numbers following fires. Stone and Juhren[1] have shown that at least for *Rhus ovata* heat is the factor responsible for the fire-induced germination. It is interesting to note that this method has been found useful in Australia in germinating some of their plants.

In the case of a few plants there is still another factor which is important and that is light. From the work so far done it appears that of the native plants, seeds of *Lobelia splendens* and some species of Mimulus must have light in order to germinate. Seeds of the common Jimson Weed *(Datura stramonium)* on the other hand fail to germinate in the presence of light. If the gardener realizes that light may be a factor in seed germination, he will be better able to understand the results which he may obtain. In the case of Mimulus and Lobelia, both of which have small seeds, it is often the practice to merely press the seed into the soil and not to cover them at all. Thus in this case the grower is unwittingly providing the seed with the light needed.

A word should be said regarding a factor which may account for poor germination of seeds of at least some species and that is that the seeds lack viable embryos. This is often true of seeds of Juniperus, the Big-leaf Maple *(Acer macrophyllum)* and Woolly Blue Curls *(Trichostema lanatum)* and may explain why the percentage of germination is often so low in these species.

Seed Composts

While different species may require very different soil mixtures for optimum growth, certain basic potting mixtures appear to give good results with seeds of many plants. It may be said that in general a seed compost should be light and well aerated yet have good moisture-retaining capacity, and at the same time, it should also contain the nutrients necessary for growth of the young plants. However, the latter point may not be of great significance since in recent years it has been found possible to start seeds in inert materials and then add the food necessary for growth of the young plants by watering the seedlings with nutrient solutions. It should be stressed that fertilizers should never be added to mixtures used for germinating seeds of native plants.

Of the many soil mixtures which have been used for starting seeds, the one recommended by the world-renowned John Innes Horticultural Institution in England has been generally accepted by many growers. It consists of a mixture of 2 parts of loam and one part each of peat (or leaf-mold) and sand. However, it is difficult to recommend a definite soil mix for general use because of the great differences found in various loams. For example, sand is often recommended for lightening soil, yet if sand is added to many of the heavy soils found in California, the resultant mixture when dry is almost as hard as cement. In general many of the California soils need to have humus added to them and this can be done by mixing in leaf-mold or peat moss and then sand or some of the spongy inert materials which are on the market under various trade names can be added to give lightness to the mixture.

At the Rancho Santa Ana Botanic Garden it has been found that many seeds germinate well in a mixture of ½ sandy loam, ¼ peat and ¼ Sponge-Rok[2]. This mixture is placed in the flat and a layer of finely chopped sphagnum moss about one-half inch thick is placed over it and the seeds then planted on sphagnum. Small seeds are merely pressed in while larger ones are covered with more sphagnum. Results following the use of this mixture

[1]E. C. Stone and G. Juhren. *The effect of fire on the germination of the seed of Rhus ovata Wats.* Amer. Jour. Bot. 38: 368-372. 1951.

[2]Manufactured by Paramount Perlite Co., Paramount, California.

have been excellent. The seedlings develop good root systems and are easily transplanted since the smaller roots are not broken in pricking-out the way they may be in many soil mixtures. Fewer seedlings have been lost from damping-off than has been the case with other mixtures. Still another advantage of this mixture is that it can be kept at an optimum moisture level rather easily. For very slow growing plants it may be necessary to feed the seedlings with a fertilizer in order to grow them large enough to transplant.

The Division of Plant Pathology of the University of California at Los Angeles has worked for a number of years on developing a mix which would be satisfactory for starting a large number of species and which could be sterilized by steam without deleterious effects. The mixture that they now advocate is called the U.C. Soil Mix. As mentioned earlier, one of the biggest difficulties in using the various soil mixtures is the great differences in the "base soil" in different areas. The loam used in the John Innes mix is usually a medium to heavy loam obtained by composting the top layer of grassland. As Dr. Chandler brought out in his paper[1] this type of loam usually contains considerable partially decomposed organic matter and a fair percentage of clay particles. The U.C. Soil Mix uses as a base wind-blown sand such as is found in many coastal areas. These sands are often quite uniform in particle size. The sand provides drainage yet holds moisture rather well. To the sand then is added peat moss, crushed rock, and nutrients. The ordinary Canadian, German, or Danish peat has been found to be quite satisfactory. The peat helps to aerate the mixture and at the same time to hold considerable water. The crushed rock is added to improve the physical character of the mix by promoting better drainage and aeration. The crushed rock should be in sizes up to ¼-¾ inches in diameter, or pea gravel about the same size may be used.

The nutrients are added by using a complete base fertilizer (2 parts by weight of superphosphate, 2 parts hoof and horn meal or grist, ½ part sulphate of potash). Calcium is added in the form of oyster shell lime.

To prepare the U.C. Soil Mix, use 7 parts by volume of base soil, 3 parts peat moss, 2 parts crushed rock. To each bushel of the mix add 8 ounces of the base fertilizer and 1½ ounces of oyster shell lime.

This mixture can be sterilized by steam without damage and is one of the reasons for its great value. While the Rancho Santa Ana Botanic Garden has not tried this mixture, it would appear that native plants would do well in it.

Transplanting

Seedlings grown in flats usually will require transplanting to individual containers before they are set out into the garden. Penstemons, Diplacus and most of the perennials are relatively easy to transplant when they are small and they can be moved as soon as they are large enough to handle, i.e. about an inch tall. Iris should not be disturbed before they are about 2 to 3 inches tall. In general, plants with a fibrous root-system transplant fairly readily when small and will usually give little trouble. On the other hand, seedlings which early develop a long strong tap-root may be rather difficult to move unless it is done before the tap-root has developed greatly. Among the plants for which this is true are the lupines, pines, oaks, etc. In some instances it is probably better to plant the seeds of these species directly into 4-inch pots or gallon cans so that the root system need not be disturbed before they are placed in the garden. In the case of species with long tap roots, it is important that everything be done to prevent the root from becoming coiled in the pots or cans.

In the case of most plants, transplanting into larger pots or gallon cans or from cans into the garden should be done before they become root-bound. This is especially important for conifers, oaks, Cercidium and Prunus, which if once root-bound never develop properly even after being planted in the garden.

---

[1] Philip A. Chandler, *The U.C. Soil Mix,* Pacific Coast Nurseryman 11: 15, 40-42, Jan. 1952.

Damping-Off

The most common cause of loss of plants in the seedling stage is a disease called damping-off. This trouble is well-known to all gardeners and in the case of native plants it can be very serious, since it appears that a number of the natives are very susceptible to the organisms which cause this disease. Among the natives, Ceanothi, Carpenteria, Fremontia, Diplacus, and Penstemon have appeared to be the most often affected.

This disease may be caused by any one of a number of fungi which are commonly found in soils all over the world. The fungus kills the tissues of the young plant at or near the ground-line and the seedlings suddenly fall.

Plant pathologists have long studied this disease and have attempted to find ways to prevent or control it. Since the causative organisms occur naturally in most soils it has been suggested that soil used for starting seedlings be sterilized. Large plant-growing establishments have special sterilizers for this purpose which use either steam or electricity and sterilize several bushels of soil at a time. Recently volatile chemicals have also been used with good results. It is possible, however, for the home gardener to sterilize all the soil needed for seed composts easily and rapidly right at home. To do this, about one-half inch of water is placed in the bottom of a large saucepan and the pan filled with dust-dry soil which has been sifted to remove stones and lumps. The mixture is brought to a boil and the heat then decreased and the mixture allowed to simmer for fifteen minutes. The soil should next be emptied onto a clean surface to allow the excess water to evaporate, after which it is ready to use.

The disease-producing fungi may also be carried by old seed flats and, therefore, used flats should be sterilized by soaking them for a time in a solution of formaldehyde and water. The flat should be allowed to dry thoroughly before using.

Another factor in preventing damping-off is to avoid planting the seeds too thickly, since a flat with a heavy stand of seedlings is much more susceptible to the disease than one where the seedlings are well spaced. It is also known that high air humidity and high soil temperature coupled with excessive water definitely favor the organisims causing damping-off. It has been suggested that, if possible, the flats be watered only on a rising temperature, preferably in the morning. Another suggestion is that the flats be thoroughly watered at the time when the seed is planted and then not moistened again until the seedlings appear.

Once damping-off occurs it is sometimes very difficult to prevent the death of a large percentage of the seedlings. Recent tests have shown that oxyquinoline sulphate and oxyquinoline benzoate are both effective in controlling the disease even after it has made its appearance in the flat. Copper oxalate sprinkled on the soil has also been used to control the disease. If the seedlings are not too small it is sometimes possible to save many of them by transplating to individual containers.

Seed treatments are also used to prevent this disease and there are a number of materials on the market which are used for this purpose.

One cultural method which has been very successful in decreasing losses due to damping-off is planting the seed in a layer of sphagnum moss which has been placed over the soil mix in the flats. This method is described in detail earlier in this chapter under seed composts.

It is believed that if the following recommendations are followed losses from damping-off may be prevented or kept at a minimum:

1. Sterilize soil which is to be used in seed composts
2. Sterilize seed flats
3. Water flats and seedlings only when absolutely necessary, then on a rising temperature
4. Plant seed in sphagnum moss as described earlier
5. Avoid high air humidity and soil temperatumes if possible
6. Do not sow seed thickly

Asexual Propagation

Asexual propagation means the reproduction of plants by means other than seed. It may include cuttings, either stem or root, dividing of old plants, grafting, or by bulbs which may be increased either by off-sets or in the case of lilies by removing scales from the bulbs, each of which then produces a new plant. While there are other methods, those listed above are the ones which are of greatest importance in propagating California natives.

There are a number of reasons why asexual propagation may be desirable. In some species it is easier or faster to divide old plants or to grow new ones from cuttings than by growing them from seed. Another reason is that some plants will not come true from seed. This is especially true in the case of hybrids; a very good example of which is to be found in the Ceanothi where hybridization occurs frequently both in the garden and in the wild. Therefore, if an especially fine hybrid Ceanothus is to be propagated it can be done only by asexual propagation, in this case by cuttings.

There are other plants such as Toyon, Carpenteria, etc. which, while they do not hybridize, vary considerably in plant form, flower size and color, fruit size, etc.; and if possible plants for the garden should only be propagated from specimens having the desired characteristics.

Propagating Frames

Except for a few plants such as willows and ocotillo, which will root and grow if placed directly in the ground, it is necessary to have some sort of a propagating frame for growing plants from cuttings. As brought out earlier, one of the simplest forms is merely a box with a few holes in the bottom and a pane of glass over the top. This frame is then partially filled with a rooting mixture into which the cuttings are placed. However, except for some of the more easily rooted species a more elaborate cutting frame is usually needed.

Control of temperature is a very important factor and the temperature inside the frame should be maintained as evenly as possible. In southern California where temperatures may vary greatly it is important that the frame be insulated to minimize temperature fluctuations. This is often done by sinking the frame in the ground with only a few inches of it extending above the surface of the soil. Another plan is to build the frame inside a greenhouse where temperature can be controlled.

While different species may have different optimum temperatures for root formation, a soil temperature of from 65-70°F. has been shown to be successful for many plants. For some cuttings bottom-heat is recommended. For the average gardener probably the easiest method is to lay electric heating cables in the bottom of the frame.

Another important factor in the rooting of cuttings is atmospheric humidity which should be sufficient to prevent the cuttings from drying out while at the same time not high enough to allow the development of fungi which would rot the material. Atmospheric humidity can be controlled to a certain extent by occasionally sprinkling the inside of the frame with a fine spray. It is important that the sash covering the frame fit tightly in order to maintain the humidity.

Control of light is also important; and in the case of outdoor cutting frames the glass sash should be whitewashed to cut down the amount of light inside the frame. At times it may also be necessary to place burlap and lath or similar materials over the glass in addition to the whitewash. Propagating frames built inside a greenhouse will usually not need whitewash if the house is shaded.

Rooting Mixtures

Sand has probably been used for rooting cuttings more than any other material. This sand should be clean and sharp, fine enough to retain moisture yet coarse enough to allow adequate drainage and aeration. It should be free from debris, especially plant materials, since decaying substances promote the growth of fungi and bacteria which may cause the cuttings to rot. In order to destroy any fungi which may be present the sand should be sterilized before it is used a second time. This may be accomplished by heating it in an oven for a period of time, making certain that the heat penetrates the entire mass.

For the rooting of many cuttings a mixture of sand and peat moss in equal parts has often been found to be superior to either sand or peat alone. One probable reason is that there is better aeration in the peat-sand mixture than in pure sand. The peat-sand mixture also has increased water-holding capacity over pure sand. Numerous other materials have also been used among which may be mentioned Vermiculite[1], Perlite[2], Sponge-Rok[3], and sphagnum moss. At the Rancho Santa Ana Botanic Garden the best results have been obtained by using a mixture of ¾ Sponge-Rok and ¼ peat moss. The use of pure sand has not been successful here but this is probably due to the type of sand used which appears to be too fine and also to contain considerable foreign matter. A cleaner and coarser type such as some of the Monterey sands would probably produce better results.

Root-Inducing Chemicals

Since 1934 when the first of the root-inducing chemicals was discovered much work has been done with these substances and at the present time the literature on the subject is voluminous. Of the materials used, it has been definitely shown that indole-3-acetic acid, indole-3-butyric acid and naphthalene-acetic acid induce root formaiton when applied to cuttings of many species of plants; and today these root-inducing substances are on the market bearing a variety of trade names.

A careful survey of the literature of the effects of these materials when used on California natives, especially the trees and shrubs, shows that almost without exception few or no beneficial results were obtained. However, this does not mean that some propagators have not been successful in using these chemicals on natives and many of them will tell you that at least at times treated cuttings rooted much better than untreated. This is not difficult to explain. At the present our knowledge concerning propagation of native plants by means of cuttings is so meager that we are in no position to evaluate correctly the effects of these root-inducing substances.

It seems best then to say that root-inducing substances have proven of value in rooting cuttings of many plants and that they may be useful in propagating California trees and shrubs, but at the present time no definite recommendations can be made. Gardeners who wish to use these chemicals should experiment with the different compounds, trying the treatments for varying lengths of time, etc., to determine which treatment is most effective under their conditions. While both liquid and powder forms are available, the powders are somewhat easier to use.

Cuttings

Cuttings may either be made from portions of the stem or from pieces of roots, the former being the commoner. However, among California natives there is one species that is readily propagated by root-cuttings and that is the Matilija Poppy. Since this is the only species in which this method is used, the details will be given later when the plant is discussed.

Stem cuttings may be classified as herbaceous, semi-hardwood or hardwood. Herbaceous cuttings are made from soft tissues such as are used for propagating geraniums. In the case of native plants this type of cutting is seldom if ever used.

Semi-hardwood cuttings are made from partially matured sections of the current season's growth. It is best to use stem tips if possible; however, sections below the tip can be used.

[1]Manufactured by Gladding McBean Co., Los Angeles, California
[2]Manufactured by Ceres of California, Paramount, California
[3]Manufactured by Paramount Perlite Co., Paramount, California

In propagating Ceanothi, Wilfrid Sheat[1] suggests using heel cuttings. It has often been recommended that the wood should be matured sufficiently so that it snaps clean when broken. This rule cannot be depended upon entirely, since there are species in which stems will not snap even though the wood is completely mature.

After the cuttings have been made, the lower leaves are removed before they are placed in the propagating frame. Formerly it was the practice to remove or trim many of the remaining leaves in order to cut down transpiration, however, at the present time the trend is to leave as many of the leaves as possible. The cuttings should be taken in the morning while the stems are still turgid. After the cuttings are in the frame they should be shaded and the atmospheric humidity maintained high enough to keep them from wilting. For certain of the natives the humidity may be kept somewhat lower than that customarily used for rooting many of the exotics, since natives appear to be very susceptible to rotting. As said before, the temperature should be maintained as nearly uniform as possible.

If only small numbers of cuttings are to be rooted they may be placed in regular greenhouse flats or even clay pots which are then placed in the frame. If pots are used, many cuttings can be rooted by merely covering the pots with a large bell-jar.

It is very difficult to recommend a definite time of year when cuttings should be taken, since environmental factors vary so much that the same stage of maturity of the new growth may be reached at very different times. In general, early spring is a favorable time for many of the California trees and shrubs. However, a few days of hot weather early in the season may mature the wood so much that material taken after that time may root very poorly. Likewise a period of hot weather coming during the time when the cuttings are in the frame may cause the temperature to become so high that the cuttings are injured.

Another important class of cuttings is the hard-wood. These may, in the case of deciduous plants, be taken during the winter when the plants are dormant to shortly before they resume growth in the spring. In the case of evergreens the cuttings are taken from mature wood. Hardwood cuttings have not been used to any great extent in the propagation of natives at this Botanic Garden. There are, nevertheless, a number of plants which can be grown very easily by this method, among which may be mentioned the Cottonwood, Chilopsis, Sycamore, Ribes and Ocotillo. Cuttings from the first four may be taken during the winter or early spring while the plants are dormant. Cuttings of Ocotillo may be made at nearly any time of year.

Bulbs

While bulb-producing plants can usually be propagated from seed, it often takes a number of years to grow plants large enough to bloom. It is therefore usually both faster and easier to propagate either from the small bulblets which are produced around the base of the old bulb, as is true of the Brodiaeas and some of the Calochorti, or as in the case of lilies to grow new plants from scales of the old bulb.

Small bulblets require no special cultural care. However, it is often advantageous to plant them in small specially prepared beds which can be protected from rodents. The bulbs can then be allowed to remain in these beds until they are large enough to flower.

Propagation of lilies from scales has long been practiced and presents no special troubles. Bulbs can be dug anytime from blooming to maturity and the outer scales snapped as close to the base of the bulb as possible. A sufficient number of scales must be allowed to remain on the old bulb to insure its growth when replanted. The scales should then be thoroughly dusted with Arasan, planted in a flat (preferably rather deep) in a mixture of ⅔ sand and ⅓ peat moss, and covered with from ¾ to 1 inch of the sand and peat mixture. The flats are placed in a greenhouse or if that is not possible in an ordinary storeroom where the temperature remains between 60-70°F. at night.

A light sandy soil can also be used in place of the sand-peat mixture in which case the

---

[1] Wilfrid Sheat. *Propagation of Trees, Shrubs and Conifers*, Macmillan & Co., London, 1951.

young plants can be allowed to complete their first year's growth in the flats without being disturbed. The flats should be watched closely in order not to allow them to become dry. The time necessary for the scales to produce small bulblets varies, but at the end of two months many of them should show growth. From the flats the young plants should be treated the same as those grown from seed. In most cases they should be placed in a frame and allowed to remain about two years before planting in the garden. One important factor must be kept in mind in propagating lilies from scales and that is a virus disease, "lily mosaic," which is responsible for a great many losses in lilies. If the plants from which the scales are taken are diseased, the plants grown from the scales will also be diseased. Therefore, scales should be used only in cases where it is known that the plants are healthy and virus-free.

Division

Many plants can be propagated easily and quickly by dividing old plants. When this method is possible it is probably to be recommended above all others. Among the California natives which can be increased in this way are the irises, *Mimulus cardinalis, Agave shawii, Calycanthus occidentalis, Lonicera involucrata,* cacti such as Echinocereus, many succulents, ferns and others. Division is usually most successful when carried out just prior to active growth in early spring.

Grafting

Grafting is a popular method for propagating many kinds of ornamental trees and shrubs, but it has never been employed to any great extent in growing California natives. Van Rensselaer and McMinn in their book on Ceanothus[1] report an attempt to graft the attractive San Diego Ceanothus *(Ceanothus cyaneus)* onto the sturdy rootstock of *C. spinosis* by inarching, a slow and difficult method. Plants grafted in this way were quite unsuccessful when grown at this Botanic Garden since strong winds broke the plants at the junction of the graft.

One interesting example of grafting used most successfully is in the case of the "Modesto Ash" which is often used as a street tree. Since male, or staminate, trees do not produce seeds and are therefore more desirable for street planting than are the seed-producing pistillate trees, cuttings from staminate plants of *Fraxinus velutina* var. *coriacea* are grafted onto rootstocks of the same species which have been grown from seed.

It is entirely possible that in the future grafting may be used in propagating more of the native trees, but as yet little work has been done in the use of this method and therefore no recommendations can be made.

---

[1]Maunsell Van Rensselaer, and Howard E. McMinn, *Ceanothus,* Santa Barbara Botanic Garden, 1942

V. RECOMMENDED SPECIES
1. Annuals

DESERT SAND VERBENA   10 inches   *Abronia villosa*

DESCRIPTION: A much-branched trailing annual covered with long glandular hairs; leaves opposite, ovate to elliptical, ½-1¼ in. long, pairs of leaves often very unequal in size and sometimes almost free from hairs on the upper surface; flowers Verbena-like, borne in few-to-many-flowered clusters at the ends of flower-stalks ⅓ in. long, flowers about ½-¾ in. long, purplish-rose in color; fruit ¼-½ in. long with 3-4 wings.

DISTRIBUTION: Found in open sandy places in the Mojave and Colorado deserts, east to Arizona and north to Utah.

PROPAGATION: By seed which may either be sown in pots and the young plants later moved to their permanent location or it can be sown directly in the ground where the plants are to bloom. Better results are probably obtained by the latter method. The first seedlings will appear in about three weeks but germination continues for some time after that. Since a high percentage of germination is rarely attained, a larger quantity of seed should be planted than would otherwise be necessary. This plant grows best in a very light and sandy loam although it can be raised rather successfully in a wide variety of soils.

Abronia villosa

27

Uses: *Abronia villosa* is very useful for giving bright summer color to dry banks, walls, etc. The only possible objection to it is that its leaves with their sticky glandular hairs may catch dust and debris.

Of the native species, *Abronia villosa* is probably the most desirable from the horticultural standpoint and little trouble will be experienced in growing it if it is planted in a sunny location in light soil. While this plant can be grown in other places, it does best in the interior where there is considerable heat and this annual should not be attempted in the cooler coastal regions. If the plants are given a small amount of water they will continue to bloom over a very long period of time.

This is the Verbena which blooms so profusely in the Palm Springs area during years when there has been sufficient moisture for its growth and during such times the desert may be covered for miles with blankets of fragrant rosy-purple flowers.

According to Bailey, *Abronia villosa* was introduced into cultivation in 1891.

There are a number of other species of Abronia native to California, the one that is best known to gardeners being *Abronia umbellata,* the common Rose-colored Sand Verbena which is found along the seashore from Los Angeles County north as far as Washington. According to some authorities *A. umbellata* was the first California plant to be grown in the Old World, having been collected by Collignon at Monterey in 1786. The garden culture for this species is the same as for *A. villosa* and for coastal areas this species is recommended instead of *A. villosa.*

There is also a yellow-flowered perennial species, *A. latifolia* which is found along the coast from Santa Barbara County north to British Columbia.

GOLD FIELDS   12 inches   *Baeria maritima*

Description: A low, branching annual from a few inches to one foot tall, forming a rounded mound if grown singly or a low mat when crowded, plants light green, somewhat succulent and hairy; leaves opposite, strap-shaped, 1/4-1/2 in. wide and 1/3 in. long, usually with 2-several small spreading lobes on either side of the leaf; flower-heads about 3/4 inch broad, borne on stems 1/3 in. long, the head little above the upper leaves, flower-heads with from 11-15 yellow rays which are about 1/4 in. long and 2-3 toothed at the tip, disk-flowers 75-100; achenes black, hairy. (An achene is a small, dry, 1-seeded fruit produced by members of the Sunflower Family.)

Distribution: *Baeria maritima* is found in coastal areas from Monterey County north as far as Vancouver Island.

Propagation: By seeds which may be planted either in late fall or early spring in the open ground where they are to bloom. Under favorable conditions germination usually takes place within a few days. Fall-sown seed will begin to flower in April and the plants will continue to bloom over a period of about two months. By early summer they may be replaced by summer- and fall-blooming plants. This species does well in heavy soil, and if occasionally watered the blooming season may be prolonged.

Uses: *Baeria maritima* is one of the easiest-grown of our annuals and is a valuable plant for use where a low yellow-flowered ground cover is wanted in early spring. It is admirably suited for filling-in between plantings of iris or other herbaceous perennials, and in areas which are not disturbed it will become naturalized and produce a low mat of yellow flowers each spring.

Gold Fields have apparently been little used by gardeners either in this country or in Europe, although several closely related species were grown in England in the early eighteen hundreds.

Baeria maritima

DESERT MARIGOLD   18 inches   *Baileya multiradiata*

DESCRIPTION: A low densely white-woolly plant 6-18 in. tall, here treated as an annual although in nature it may be perennial; stems several to many from the base; leaves mostly basal, alternate, lower ones lobed, upper ones with few or no lobes; flower-heads 1-1¾ in. in diameter, borne on stalks 6-18 in. long, ray-flowers 20-50, rays about ½ in. long, bright yellow when young, lighter in age, disk-flowers numerous, yellow.

DISTRIBUTION: *Baileya multiradiata* occurs on sunny rocky slopes and mesas in the eastern Mojave Desert, east as far as Texas and north to Utah. It is also found in Mexico.

PROPAGATION: By seed which may be sown in the open ground in March and April or the plants may be started in flats and later transplanted. A rocky or sandy well-drained soil is best, although they can be grown in heavier soil if extreme care is taken to avoid over-watering since the plants are very subject to crown-rot when grown under wet conditions. Later plantings made in June or even July, if watered occasionally, will produce plants which bloom freely in late summer and during the fall when there are few other natives in flower.

USES: *Baileya multiradiata* is a species which can be highly recommended to give an abundance of bloom over a long period. The plants with their low woolly gray leaves and one-foot flower-stalks each topped by a head of golden flowers constitute a very good subject for bedding purposes in dry well-drained soils. It has been successfully used for growing along dry road banks and in traffic islands of divided highways. It is especially useful for the latter purpose since it needs little attention and volunteers readily.

When this plant was introduced into cultivation is not known. It was first grown at this Botanic Garden in 1935 from seed collected in the Clark Mountains. Since that time it has been used regularly at the Garden where its attractive yellow flowers and its long period of bloom have caused comment by many visitors. It is also reported to be grown to a limited extend in southeastern United States.

TURKISH RUGGING   10 inches   *Chorizanthe staticoides*

DESCRIPTION: A low intricately branched annual 4-10 in. tall, entire plant reddish-purple; leaves basal, oblong to elliptical, green above, hairy on the lower side, ¼-1¼ in. long; flowers small, rose-colored, borne in dense clusters at the tips of the much-branched stems.

DISTRIBUTION: *Chorizanthe staticoides* is found on dry slopes and flats from Riverside and the Santa Ana Mts. north to Santa Barbara and central California.

PROPAGATION: Turkish Rugging is propagated by seed which should be sown in late fall or early spring where the plants are to bloom. Germination takes place within a few weeks. This species prefers a coarse well-drained soil although it can be grown in other soils fairly well.

USES: Turkish Rugging cannot be recommended for general garden planting. Due to the unusual raspberry color of the plants it is most attractive in masses seen at a distance and it can be used to good advantage as a low colorful ground cover in rather dry sterile soils. The plants are also useful for covering dry banks or in large open spots where mass effect is desirable.

Nothing is known about the horticultural history of this plant.

Chorizanthe staticoides

Baileya multiradiata

31

Clarkia elegans

CLARKIA 2 feet *Clarkia elegans*

DESCRIPTION: An erect annual 1-5 feet tall (usually about 2 ft.), often sparingly branched; leaves alternate, 1-1¾ in. long, egg-shaped to oblong egg-shaped, edges of the leaves either smooth or irregularly set with small teeth; flowers rose to purple, borne singly in the axis of the upper leaves, flowers composed of 5 petals which are about ½-¾ in. long, the lower half being narrow and strap-like, the upper half broad and somewhat triangular in shape; seed capsules usually curved and covered with hairs. Botanically this plant is now correctly known as *Clarkia unguiculata.*

DISTRIBUTION: According to Harlan Lewis this species is "almost inevitably found growing in oak or oak-digger pine woodland" and is distributed in California from Butte and Mendocino counties south to San Diego County.

PROPAGATION: By seed which should be sown during the late fall or in the early spring. The plants thrive best in a rather light soil but will grow under a wide variety of conditions. However, if the soil is too rich the plants become tall and spindly and produce relatively few flowers. The young plants should be pinched back in order to increase branching.

Uses: Clarkias vary considerably in nature in flower color, size, and plant form. The European horticulturists noting these variations selected and saved the more attractive forms and thus within a few years they were able to offer gardeners a great many varieties varying in color from pure white through shades of salmon and pink to deep purple. Double-flowered forms were also developed. Something of the quality of many of these early selections may be seen when it is realized that a number of them are still being offered for sale some eighty years after their introduction. For garden use the selected horticultural strains are recommended rather than the wild forms which for the most part are of inferior color, size, and habit to those of the named varieties.

Clarkias are certainly among the best known of all the California annuals and they are found in gardens in many parts of the world. *Clarkia elegans* was introduced into cultivation in England about 1832 from seed collected by David Douglas somewhere in California. Douglas also introduced another species *Clarkia pulchella,* a plant which he collected in Oregon in 1825. Few plants have ever become popular with gardeners faster than did the Clarkias. Within eight years after Douglas made his first collection of *Clarkia pulchella,* the English botanist, Lindley, described it as "that sweet North American flower that in a few years has changed from an obscure Botanical rarity to the ornament of every flower-market from London and Paris to Moscow and Stockholm."

COREOPSIS 12 inches *Coreopsis calliopsidea*

DESCRIPTION: An erect, usually rather stout annual 6-12 in. tall with several stems from a taproot, stems yellow-green, usually leafy to the middle or above, occasionally branching near the base; leaves somewhat fleshy, divided into linear segments which have blunt tips; flower-heads erect, solitary at the tips of the branches, large, 1-2 in. in diameter with about 8 yellow rays, however, the number of rays varies considerably and some flowers may be semi-double, disk-flowers golden yellow; achenes dark brown, shining.

DISTRIBUTION: *Coreopsis calliopsidea* is found in the western part of the Mojave Desert, in San Bernardino and Kern counties, west to San Luis Obispo County and north as far as Alameda County.

PROPAGATION: By seeds which should be sown during late fall or early spring where they are to bloom. The seeds germinate in from two weeks to a month and the plants will begin to bloom in late February or early March from fall-sown seed and will continue in flower for about two months. Care should be taken in watering the plants since excessive water tends to promote root rot.

USES: This Coreopsis can be highly recommended as an early blooming, yellow-flowered, low bedding plant. However, it finishes flowering early enough so that it may be replaced with later-blooming ones.

Grown side by side in rather heavy soil at the Botanic Garden, *C. calliopsidea* has been more successful than *C. bigelovii. C. calliopsidea* also produces larger flowers and for those reasons it is recommended rather than *bigelovii* which is more often encountered in gardens.

Nothing is known regarding the horticultural history of this species.

Besides *C. bigelovii* there is still another annual Coreopsis which is sometimes grown as a garden plant. *Coreopsis stillmanii* is a stoutish plant 9-12 in. tall with orange-yellow flowers. It is found on the western side of the Sierra Nevada from Butte County to Tulare County and on the eastern side of the South Coast Ranges in Contra Costa, Santa Clara, and Stanislaus counties. This species has not been grown at this Botanic Garden but it is reported to do best in a sandy soil. English catalogues list a double-flowered form under the name of *Leptosyne stillmanii* 'Golden Rosette'.

33

CALIFORNIA POPPY   18 inches   *Eschscholzia californica*

DESCRIPTION: A leafy perennial here treated as an annual, much-branched from the base, forming a rounded clump up to 18 in. in height and equally broad; leaves much-divided, the ultimate segments linear or oblong, the entire leaf sometimes 1 ft. long, green to blue-green in color; flowers large, more or less bowl-shaped with a conspicuous collar-like ring below the flower, petals ½-2 in. long, color yellow to deep orange but extremely variable.

DISTRIBUTION: *Eschscholzia californica* is common in valleys and on hills throughout much of California.

PROPAGATION: By seeds which should be sown in late fall or early spring where the plants are to bloom. The California Poppy is not particular as to soil, however, it does best in a light sandy loam and it should be given full sun.

USES: The California Poppy was noted by all the early explorers who came to California and much has been written about this interesting and beautiful plant. It was introduced into Europe by Douglas and is probably the most widely grown of all California natives, being known in practically all temperate parts of the world. It has in fact become a weed in some areas in Europe, India, and Australia.

During its long history as a cultivated plant the California Poppy has been subjected to much selection for color and, to a lesser degree, for plant habit with the result that today there are on the market a great many named varieties of the species, ranging in color all the way from pale cream through buff, light yellow, golden-yellow and orange to rose and

Eschscholzia californica

red. There are also a number of varieties which have two-toned flowers, with one color on the inside of the petal and another on the outside. All of them can be grown with the greatest of ease and it is to be deplored that California gardeners do not use more of these beautiful plants.

Eschscholzia californica is not the only species of California Poppy available to gardeners and some of the small annuals are most desirable subjects for the rock garden. Eschscholzia pulchella and E. lobbii produce a low basal tuft of leaves from which extend the leafless flower-stalks, each bearing a single small yellow flower. E. caespitosa is somewhat larger and the more or less leafless flower-stalks bear pure yellow flowers with petals ½-1 inch long. The propagation and handling of these species is the same as for E. californica.

Gilia achilleaefolia

PHOTOGRAPH BY DOUGLAS EBERSOLE

GILIA   3 feet   *Gilia achilleaefolia*

DESCRIPTION: An annual 8-36 in. tall, usually with several branches; leaves mainly on the lower half of the plant but not crowded, individual leaf 1¼-4 in. long, much-divided, the ultimate segments very slender; flowers numerous, borne in dense clusters at the ends of rather long flower-stalks, individual flowers somewhat funnel-shaped, about ½ in. long, corolla pale blue with a white throat.

DISTRIBUTION: *Gilia achilleaefolia* is common on dry slopes and disturbed places along the base of the mountains below 5000 ft. from San Diego County north to central California.

PROPAGATION: By seeds which should be sown during late fall or early spring where the plants are to flower. Fall-sown seed germinates in from two to four weeks and the plants will commence flowering in March and continue for about two months.

USES: This Gilia is a most attractive blue-flowered annual which is best when massed and is therefore especially useful for bedding purposes. The flowers are good for cutting since they last well in water.

Gilia achilleaefolia is a variable species and many different forms are found in nature. The strain most grown at the Rancho Santa Ana Botanic Garden was originally obtained from Theodore Payne, who does not know the source of the seed. Dr. Verne Grant, the foremost authority on this group, after an intensive study of the various forms believes that this strain came from England and possibly has descended from seed first collected by Douglas. If this is true, Dr. Grant believes that Douglas must have collected the seed originally in the Mt. Hamilton Range.

There are other species of Gilia on the market and some of them are occasionally seen in gardens. Probably the commonest and most attractive is *Gilia tricolor* which grows 1-1½ ft. tall and has comparatively large flowers of a pale blue or lilac with a yellow throat and dark blue or purple spots. *G. tricolor* has long been grown in Europe where it was introduced by Douglas. It is most effective when grown thickly in a bed, as is true of *G. achilleaefolia*.

LARGE-FLOWERED GODETIA   2 feet   *Godetia whitneyi*

DESCRIPTION: An erect or spreading annual 1½-2 ft. tall, stems stiff, reddish or green; leaves alternate, those on the short side branches bunched, leaves 2½-4 in. long and ½-¾ in. wide, lance-shaped; flowers solitary in the upper axils but due to the shortening of the axis the flowers form a short dense inflorescence of from 4-6 flowers; buds erect, 1½ in. long, open flower 2, to as much as 4, inches in diameter, petals 4, a pale lavender to almost white with a large purplish-red blotch at the base; seed capsule about 1½ in. long, tapering toward both ends and containing numerous small brown seeds.

Godetia whitneyi is known only from a few localities along the coast in Mendocino and Humboldt counties. This plant has long been known to gardeners as *Godetia whitneyi* and it is unfortunate that the correct name for it has to be changed to *Clarkia amoena* subsp. *whitneyi*.

PROPAGATION: By seed which may be sown in the open either in late fall or early spring. At the Botanic Garden it has been found that the fall plantings generally give better results. If desired the plants may also be started in flats and later transplanted. Godetias can be grown in nearly any soil, but as with the Clarkias if the soil is too rich the plants become rank and floppy. In any case they should be given a sunny location. Thorough irrigation at intervals until the plants begin to flower will insure large vigorous plants, however, after they have once begun to flower watering should be reduced. If the seed is sown in the open ground the plants should be thinned to one to two feet. It is also advisable to pinch plants back in order to induce branching.

USES: California contains a number of species of Godetia and many of them were introduced into cultivation early in the last century. Like the Clarkias they quickly became popular garden annuals and have been grown extensively since that time. *Godetia whitneyi*, however, was not one of the first to be introduced since it was not known until 1867 when the botanist, H. N. Bolander found it at Shelter Cove in Humboldt County. Bolander collected seed from the plants. Some of this material he sent to England where Thompson of the Ipswich Nurseries first flowered it in 1870 under the name of *Oenothera whitneyi*.

Plant breeders early became interested in the Godetias and proceeded to hybridize the various species, later selecting from the crosses horticulturally desirable forms. Thus over a

36

period of time many new and interesting varieties were placed on the market. At the present time there are numerous named varieties and these improved forms, many of them developed from G. *whitneyi*, are recommended to gardeners as well as the species itself. In color the horticultural varieties vary from pure white to carmine with numerous shades of pink, rose, and salmon, the petals often blotched at the base with a deeper color. Double-flowered forms are also available. In size the plants vary from dwarfs less than a foot high to forms several feet tall.

Other species which are sometimes grown are *Godetia biloba (Clarkia biloba)*, a plant with small leaves and flowers, each petal of which is divided into two distinct lobes; G. *bottae (Clarkia bottae)*, which has rosy-lavender flowers covered with small purple dots; G. *cylindrica (Clarkia cylindrica)*, a much-branched plant with deep lavender flowers with deep purple spots; and G. *dudleyana (Clarkia dudleyana)* with flowers of pinkish-lavender with flecks of reddish-purple on the lower part of the petals.

Godetia whitneyi

Layia platyglossa var. *elegans*

TIDY-TIPS 18 inches *Layia platyglossa* var. *elegans*

DESCRIPTION: An erect, simple or branched annual 8-18 in. tall; leaves alternate, 1½-2¾ in. long, the basal ones narrow-oblong, toothed or divided into segments, upper leaves reduced with the uppermost narrow, lance-shaped and undivided, entire plant covered with short stiff hairs; flowers borne in heads at the ends of short flower-stalks, flower-heads 1-1¾ in. in diameter with from 5-12 rays, rays sulphur yellow commonly tipped with white, disk-flowers yellow.

DISTRIBUTION: *Layia platyglossa* var. *elegans* is found on dry flats and slopes in coastal southern California north to Napa and Mendocino counties and south into Baja California.

PROPAGATION: By seeds which may be sown during late fall or early spring where the plants are to bloom. This annual prefers a rather light sandy soil but does very well in a heavy loam if sufficient humus is available.

USES: Tidy-tips is a bright little plant and is most effective when planted thickly in beds. The flower-heads with their yellow rays, each tipped with white, make it unusual and quite different from any other California annual.

It is not known when this plant was first grown in cultivation. The Journal of the Royal Horticultural Society lists it among the species being grown at Wisley in 1889.

CALIFORNIA PHLOX 14 inches *Linanthus grandiflorus*

DESCRIPTION: A slender annual 3-14 in. tall, stems erect, simple or branched; the leaves which are often crowded immediately below the inflorescence are divided almost to

Linanthus grandiflorus

PHOTOGRAPH BY PERCY EVERETT

39

the base into narrow linear lobes ⅔-1 in. long, lower ones minutely hairy or sometimes smooth, upper ones with hairs only on edges of the leaf; flowers phlox-like, white or pink, in dense, few-to-many flowered heads.

DISTRIBUTION: *Linanthus grandiflorus* is found on open mountain slopes and valley flats from Marin and Alameda counties south to Monterey County.

PROPAGATION: By seeds which should be sown where the plants are to flower. Plants raised from fall-sown seed will generally produce flowers during April and May.

USES: California Phlox can be highly recommended for bedding purposes. If sown thickly the plants produce a solid blanket of color for about two to three months blooming well into summer if they are watered occasionally. The flower color varies from pink, pale lavender, to white.

This species has been known by gardeners for a long period, having been introduced into cultivation from seed collected by David Douglas. Unfortunately there has been considerable confusion concerning the correct name for the plant. It was first described as *Leptosiphon densiflorus*. Later this was changed to *Gilia densiflora*, but today it is properly known as *Linanthus grandiflorus*. However in horticultural literature and in many seed catalogues it is still offered as *Gilia densiflora* or California Phlox. Regardless of the name under which it is listed, this lovely California annual is highly recommended as an early spring bedding plant.

Another species, *Linanthus dianthiflorus* (also known as *Gilia dianthoides*) is a very lovely, low-growing annual 2-6 inches high. When covered with rose or lilac-colored flowers, it is an extremely attractive little plant worthy of a place in any garden; however its low compact nature makes it especially desirable for the rock garden. *L. dianthiflorus*, however, cannot be whole-heartedly recommended because of the erratic way it behaves. Here at the Garden one year it germinated well and produced quantities of low rounded plants completely covered with flowers, while the following season it was practically impossible to germinate the seeds. Nevertheless for the gardener who likes to experiment with the more difficult species, this plant is highly recommended. It was first discovered by Douglas and introduced into England through seed collected by William Lobb.

ANNUAL LUPINE   12 inches   *Lupinus nanus*

DESCRIPTION: A low annual often branching at the base, stems 8-12 inches tall, hairy; leaves composed of from 5-7, linear to oblanceolate leaflets, ⅝-1¼ in. long, pubescent on both surfaces, and occurring at the end of a long petiole; flowers borne in elongated clusters, individual flowers pea-shaped, ⅜-⅝ in. long, blue (or sometimes white or pink); seed pod ¾-1½ in. long, hairy.

DISTRIBUTION: *Lupinus nanus* is native from northern California south to northern Santa Barbara County and on the north slopes of the Tehachapi Mts.

PROPAGATION: By seeds which, since lupines are difficult to transplant, should be sown where the plants are to flower. They thrive best in a light, well-drained soil in full sun. As in the case of other species of lupines the percentage of germination may be low due to the presence of so-called "hard seeds." Methods for overcoming this condition are described in the chapter on seed germination.

USES: Planted in masses *Lupinus nanus* produces an abundance of color over a period of about two months during the spring and it is considered most effective when used as a low bedding plant or ground cover.

Douglas introduced *Lupinus nanus* into cultivation, in England, in 1833. The color varies, as in the case of many lupines, both pink and albino forms being known and available from English seed firms.

There are a number of other species of annual lupine which are occasionally cultivated

Lupinus benthami

Lupinus succulentus

in gardens. *Lupinus succulentus,* a blue-flowered (or pink) species found in ravines, on hillsides and in fields and along roadsides of much of California, is one of the most easily grown species, but it may be considered somewhat coarse for most gardens. *L. benthami* is a most attractive species with deep blue flowers borne on long flower-stalks well above the leaves, but unfortunately it is somewhat more difficult to handle in the garden than *L. nanus.* One of the most unusual little annual species is *L. stiversi* which often reaches only a few inches in height. The flowers are a pleasing combination of yellow and pink or purple. Found in sand and gravel, it is rather difficult to grow but is highly recommended for use in rock gardens where its cultural requirements can be met. *L. hirsutissimus* has amaranth-red flowers and leaves with stiff nettle-like hairs. It occurs naturally in loose gravelly soil in hot dry places in the hills from San Mateo County south to Baja California.

The bush lupines are described under "shrubs."

BLAZING STAR 4 feet *Mentzelia lindleyi*

DESCRIPTION: A large erect annual 1-4 ft. tall, simple or branching, plant covered with short barbed hairs; leaves alternate, oval to narrowly lance-shaped, the lower as much as 6-8 in. long, edges irregularly lobed or toothed, leaves harsh to the touch; flowers large and showy, in clusters of from 1-4 at the tips of short axillary branches, individual flowers about 1½ in. in diameter with 5 golden-yellow petals each with a burnt-orange spot at the base; stamens numerous, often about 100 forming a mound in the center of the flower; seed capsule about 1-2 in. long, fleshy when young, later becoming membranaceous, seeds small and numerous.

Mentzelia lindleyi

DISTRIBUTION: *Mentzelia lindleyi* is found on rocky canyon slopes in the Mt. Hamilton Range and the central Sierra Nevada foothills.

PROPAGATION: By seed which may be planted where the plants are ultimately to bloom or if desired this species can be started in flats and later transplanted. The seed, which may be sown either in late fall or very early winter, will usually germinate in from one to two weeks and plants from fall-sown seed will begin to flower in April and will continue for a period of about two months. While the plants will grow in comparatively heavy loam if it is well drained, they do best in a light sandy soil. It is important, however, that they be given full sun and if possible some water up to the time when they start to bloom. After that time watering should almost be discontinued. If grown in heavy soils excess moisture may cause them to rot.

USES: Blazing Star is one of the most attractive of the larger yellow-flowered annuals native to California and it is recommended for planting in masses in sunny gardens where a rather large, yellow-flowered, early blooming plant is desired. It cannot be recommended for the average small garden because of its size and also its rather weedy appearance when grown singly or in small numbers.

Mentzelia lindleyi (also known as *Bartonia aurea*) was introduced into cultivation in England from seed sent by Douglas in 1834. It soon became popular with the English gardeners and is still grown in that country.

FIVE-SPOT NEMOPHILA   6 inches   *Nemophila maculata*

DESCRIPTION: A low annual only a few inches high but spreading to as much as 1 ft. in diameter; leaves opposite, 1-2 in. long, light green and rather succulent, divided into 5-9 rounded lobes; flower-stalks erect, short, and bearing a single flower which may be as much as 2 in. across, petals 5, white with fine purple veins and small purple dots near the base and a single large purple spot at the tip of the petal; seed capsule spherical, about ½ in. in diameter with from 6-8 seeds.

DISTRIBUTION: *Nemophila maculata* is native to the Sierra Nevada foothills from Nevada County south to Kern County where it is found in meadows which are wet in the early spring and dry later in the season.

PROPAGATION: The seed may be planted either in rows or broadcast on loose soil during late fall. If thinned so that the plants are about one foot apart they will completely cover the ground later. They do very well in heavy soil but they should have full sun. Considerable water is needed both for the germination of the seeds and for the growth of the young plants. This species is one of the few natives which will benefit from the application of a small amount of fertilizer. However, too rich a soil reduces the number of flowers produced and will also cause the plants to become straggly and unattractive. Five-spot Nemophila produces an abundance of seed and will readily re-seed itself.

USES: *Nemophila maculata* can be recommended highly as an attractive low bedding or border plant which is easy to grow and will produce an abundance of its attractive and most unusual flowers over a period from March to May. During its blooming season this little annual is one of the most talked about plants in the garden.

It was introduced into cultivation in 1848 from seed collected by Hartweg.

Nemophila maculata

WHITE EVENING PRIMROSE

2 feet   *Oenothera deltoides* var. *cognata*

DESCRIPTION: A vigorous coarse annual 1-2 ft. tall and from 1-3 ft. across, stems pale green to whitish; leaves alternate, oblong to lance-shaped, 2-7 in. long, tapering gradually to the base, edges irregularly wavy-margined with a few coarse teeth near the base; flowers 4-petalled, white, large, 3-4 in. in diameter, borne singly in the axils of the leaves but congested at the tips of the branches, flowers white, opening late in the afternoon and remaining open until well into the following day, gradually fading to a pink before closing.

DISTRIBUTION: *Oenothera deltoides* var. *cognata* is found only in the San Joaquin Valley from Kern County to Sacramento County and the adjacent Coast Ranges where it is often known to cover large areas of sandy wastelands.

PROPAGATION: By seeds which may be planted where they are to bloom or they may be started in flats and transplanted later. Fall planting is probably best but the weather must be fairly warm to insure good germination. The seeds should be covered lightly and the soil well watered. The young plants do not develop much during the winter but with the advent of warm spring days growth is rapid and by late March the plants will begin to produce flowers and will continue to do so well into late spring and early summer.

USES: This Primrose is recommended as one of our finest white-flowered annuals. While the flowers last only a single day, they are produced in such large numbers that they present a very attractive appearance over several months. Toward the end of the season the plants become weedy in appearance and should be removed.

Oenothera deltoides var. *cognata* has been grown at the Rancho Santa Ana Botanic Garden since 1933.

Oenothera deltoides var. *cognata*

PHOTOGRAPH BY DOUGLAS EBERSOLE

Phacelia viscida

PHACELIA   12 inches   *Phacelia viscida*

DESCRIPTION: An annual 8-12 in. tall, either simple or slightly branched, entire plant pubescent with glandular hairs; leaves alternate, broadly egg-shaped to roundish, irregularly toothed, ½ to as much as 3 in. long; flowers few to many in a short terminal cluster; flowers deeply saucer-shaped, ½-¾ in. in diameter, deep blue with a white center.

DISTRIBUTION: *Phacelia viscida* is found in open ground along the coast from San Luis Obispo County south to San Diego County and Baja California.

PROPAGATION: By seeds which may be sown either during late fall or early spring in the area the plants are wanted. The seeds germinate readily and those plants from fall-sown seed will produce flowers early in March and continue to do so for about two months. While this Phacelia will grow in heavy soil it is at its best in a light loam, but regardless of the soil condition it should have full sun.

For best effect the plants should be grown as single specimens rather than planted thickly as is recommended for many of the California annuals. Since they are sometimes attacked by mildew, they should never be watered by overhead sprinkling which favors the development of that disease.

USES: *Phacelia viscida* is recommended to gardeners because of its very fine deep blue and most attractive flowers. There may, however, be some objections to the use of this plant in gardens. Some people receive a skin irritation upon contact with the plant, and these sticky annuals badly stain the hands and clothing.

2. Perennials

COLUMBINE 3 feet *Aquilegia eximia*

DESCRIPTION: An herbaceous perennial 1½-3 ft. tall, stems freely branched especially above; leaves much divided, the individual leaflets broadly oval to roundish in outline, ⅜-1½ in. long, green above, and with a whitish bloom on the underside, leaflets cut to the middle, the lobes set with pointed teeth, entire plant densely glandular-hairy; flowers borne singly on nodding stems as much as 4 in. long, sepals 5, spreading or reflexed, reddish, spurs coarse, scarlet below, yellowish near the mouth, ¾-1¼ in. long and about ⅜ in. in diameter at the opening, stamens numerous, ⅝-1 in. long.

DISTRIBUTION: *Aquilegia eximia* is found in canyons of the Coast Ranges from Mendocino County south to San Luis Obispo County.

PROPAGATION: By seed which may be sown in flats during early fall and the plants later transferred to individual containers or other flats, or the seed may be sown in prepared open ground. If the plants are set into the garden in early spring they will bloom that summer.

USES: This columbine is highly recommended for garden planting being especially useful in the perennial border, on moist banks, or along artificial streams in natural plantings. The plants do well in most types of soil, but they should not be allowed to remain dry for long periods. They can be grown fairly well in full sun, thriving better, however, in partial shade. This species is notable for its coarse spurs and the lack of a petal-blade, and for these reasons the flowers are quite different in appearance from most columbines.

Little is known regarding the horticultural history of this species. According to Munz it first bloomed in Europe in 1856.

Aguilegia eximia

PHOTOGRAPH BY E. K. BALLS

Artemisia pycnocephala

COAST SAGEBRUSH   2 feet   *Artemisia pycnocephala*

DESCRIPTION: An erect or spreading woody-based perennial 1-2 ft. tall, often as much as 2 ft. broad; leaves crowded, especially toward the base of the stems, leaves 1-2 in. long and once or twice divided, the ultimate segments long and narrow, sometimes spoon-shaped; inflorescence a narrow, erect cluster of flowers 2-4 in. wide and rising about 1 ft. above the rest of the plant, the tip of the inflorescence drooping or nodding, flower heads small, lacking the conspicuous ray-flowers which are so characteristic of members of the Sunflower Family.

DISTRIBUTION: *Artemisia pycnocephala* is found on sand hills along the coast from Monterey County north to Humboldt County.

PROPAGATION: The Coast Sagebrush is propagated by seed which is best sown in flats. Germination takes place in about two weeks, and by the end of two months the seedlings are large enough to be placed in small pots or separated into other flats. They may then be moved later to larger pots or set into the ground. The Coast Sagebrush is not particular as to soil even growing in heavy adobe if they are not given too much water. In lighter soils this species will stand moderate irrigation. Planted in the full sun this perennial makes neat, soft, silvery-gray mounds, when in shade they tend to become lax and are less gray in color.

USES: The Coast Sagebrush is probably the most attractive of all the native gray-leaved perennials and is recommended for border planting or for any sunny location where a low-growing gray-leaved plant is required. It is especially attractive when used in front of deep green-leaved shrubs. The plants should not be pruned but they can be maintained as

48

low clumps by removing the flowering stems when these appear. As they become more or less unattractive in age they should be replaced about every two years.

This species will do well in any of the coastal areas of the state but it should not be used in the hot interior valleys.

WILD GINGER 12 inches *Asarum caudatum*

DESCRIPTION: A low evergreen perennial with slender creeping rootstocks bearing 2-3 scalelike bracts, then 1-2 heart- or kidney-shaped leaves, leaves 2-6 in. broad, pubescent below, smooth above except on the veins; flowers borne singly in the axils of the lower leaves and near the ground, flowers without a corolla but the calyx corolla-like with 3 lobes which are triangular in shape and with the tip attenuated into a tail 1-2½ in. long.

DISTBIBUTION: *Asarum caudatum* is found in deep shade usually in the Redwood Belt of the Coast Ranges from the Santa Cruz Mts. north to Del Norte County.

PROPAGATION: Wild Ginger is most easily propagated by dividing old plants. They should be grown in a rich, moist soil provided with moderate to heavy shade. It is important that they be placed where they will not be in competition with other plants.

USES: While Wild Ginger is seldom grown in California, it can be recommended as a very satisfactory ground cover for areas with dense shade such as under trees. In such locations the large deep green leaves will soon form a solid mat which will remain green and attractive all year. The flowers are unimportant and may be seen only by getting down on the ground and searching among the leaves. They are, however, among the most curious flowers to be found on any of the natives.

Ararum caudatum

PHOTOGRAPH BY DOUGLAS EBERSOLE

49

There is little knowledge as to when this plant was first grown in a garden. In Nicholson's Dictionary there is a note that this is a "rare and pretty species" and the date "1880," the time they give for its introduction into horticulture.

Cirsium occidentale

WESTERN THISTLE   4 feet   *Cirsium occidentale*

DESCRIPTION: A stout erect plant 2-4 ft. tall; leaves lance-shaped or oblong, 2-10 in. long, sharply toothed and wavy-margined, entire plant silvery-gray due to a dense, soft woolly pubescence; flower-heads borne singly at the tips of the branches, heads subglobose, the involucral bracts straight and densely cobwebby, flowers crimson with a touch of purple like the flowers of the Redbud.

DISTRIBUTION: *Cirsium occidentale* is commonly found in many areas of coastal California.

PROPAGATION: By seed which may be sown where the plants are to bloom, or it may be started in flats and the seedlings transplanted to pots and later to the open ground. Seed sown in late fall will produce plants which will begin to bloom in May and continue into July. Western Thistle does best in a light, well-drained soil although it has bloomed well at the Botanic Garden where it was grown in rather heavy loam.

USES: There are few people who are not familiar with at least some of the thistles, however, there are few who know that there are species which are extremely attractive and quite desirable as garden plants. *Cirsium occidentale* is such a plant. The combination of silver-gray pubescence and purplish-crimson flowers which are surrounded by the silver-white cobweb on the involucral bracts makes this species a most unusual garden subject. Unfortunately in view of its size, the plant cannot be recommended for the small garden.

This thistle has been grown rarely, however, an English writer, Thomas Hay, in his book *Plants for the Connoisseur* writes that "A friend who recently returned from a visit to America, and whose opinion I value, told me he considers this the most desirable novelty seen in the United States, and it may easily be imagined that a large group would be most telling."

Coreopsis maritima

SEA-DAHLIA   2 feet   *Coreopsis maritima*

DESCRIPTION: A bushy perennial as much as 2 ft. tall from a slightly woody crown; leaves yellow-green, glossy, fern-like, 6-10 in. long, divided into many narrow segments, the entire leaf rather brittle and succulent; flower-heads large, 2½-4 in. in diameter, borne singly on leafless stems 12-18 in. long, ray-flowers 14-20, bright lemon-yellow.

DISTRIBUTION: *Coreopsis maritima* is a very local species known only on the bluffs along the beach from Oceanside, San Diego County south to northern Baja California and on San Martin and the Coronado Islands. The plants are usually scattered and their total number in nature is probably not great.

PROPAGATION: By seeds which germinate readily either in flats, in outdoor seed beds, or in prepared ground in the garden. If grown in flats the young seedlings should be potted in individual containers when large enough to handle. Seed sown in the fall will produce plants which will bloom the following spring, and those sown in the spring will give plants that will bloom during the fall or late summer.

This species grows best in sandy, well-drained soil that is not too rich, and water should be withheld during the summer, permitting dormancy. The plants produce tuber-like roots which may readily be transplanted.

51

Uses: The Sea-Dahlia is recommended for gardens in coastal areas or at reasonable distances inland. In locations where the plants thrive they will volunteer if the ground is not disturbed too frequently. The flowers of the Sea-Dahlia are excellent for cutting and will last for several days in water. In areas with cold winters it may be handled as an annual.

Coreopsis maritima was discovered at San Diego by Thomas Nuttall about 1835 and according to Hooker, Nuttall introduced it into American gardens. It was first grown in England about 1873.

CHALK DUDLEYA   12 inches   *Dudleya pulverulenta*

DESCRIPTION: A succulent perennial from a short thick rootstock, leaves numerous, forming a flat rosette sometimes over 12 in. in diameter; leaves light gray-green and covered with a dense coating of chalky-white powder, the amount varying with the season and age of the leaves, basal leaves 6-8 in. long and 2-3 in. wide, egg-shaped or spatulate, the tips usually with a short point; flowers borne on stalks 1-3 ft. tall, often several from a single rosette, stem leaves small and clasping, inflorescence with several branches 6-12 in. long, flowers small, drooping, deep red in color.

DISTRIBUTION: *Dudleya pulverulenta* is found in the coastal regions of southern California from San Luis Obispo County south to Baja California. It ranges inland only in the Cuyamaca Mts. in San Diego County.

Dudleya pulverulenta

PROPAGATION: The Chalk Dudleya may be propagated by seeds, or very rarely a plant is found with branches which may be removed and rooted. Older plants can be transplanted easily.

The seeds, which are very minute, should be sown in flats containing a light soil mixture which is covered with a layer of sphagnum. The seeds are distributed on the sphagnum and a piece of glass then placed over the flat. When the seedlings appear the glass should be removed. Because of the extreme fineness of the seed care should be taken not to sow it too thickly. When the seedlings have become large enough to handle they may be transplanted to individual containers or replanted in the flats. The plants will usually be large enough to place in their permanent locations in about a year.

This species grows best in coarse well-drained soil and experience at the Rancho Santa Ana Botanic Garden has shown that it is the normal position for the plants to be tilted. This permits excess water to drain off and prevents rotting of the crown and is probably one of the most important considerations in the successful culture of these plants.

USES: The Chalk Dudleya is certainly the most spectacular of the California species of Dudleya and it is most attractive when grown on rocky slopes or in association with chaparral shrubs.

Erigeron glaucus

BEACH ASTER   10 inches   *Erigeron glaucus*

DESCRIPTION: A perennial with erect stems 4-10 in. high arising from a basal tuft of leaves; leaves spatulate to egg-shaped, 1-4 in .long, margins sometime set with a small tooth on either side just below the tip, upper leaves small and scattered; flower-heads large,

53

1¼-1½ in. broad, ray-flowers numerous, narrow, relatively short, pale lavender to violet, disk-flowers numerous, yellow.

DISTRIBUTION: *Erigeron glaucus* is common on cliffs and sandy shores near the sea from Monterey County north to Humboldt County. It is also found on San Miguel Island.

PROPAGATION: The Beach Aster may be started either from seeds or cuttings. Seed sown in flats filled with a sandy soil germinates in about a week and the seedlings may be transplanted when large enough to handle to individual pots and later moved to where they are to flower. Seed can also be sown directly into the open ground. While the plants prefer a light sandy loam, from the number of volunteers which have appeared each year at the Botanic Garden it would appear that they will also grow in rather heavy loam. If watered occasionally during the summer, the plants will bloom over a long period of time.

USES: The Beach Aster can be recommended only for use in coastal areas. Inland the flowers tend to lose much of their color and often become a rather dingy white.

Little is known regarding the history of this species but introduction into cultivation was apparently quite early. The Botanical Register for 1815 reports that "It first appeared amongst us three or four years ago." However, it was not known from what country it had come and the gardener who raised it said that he was almost certain that it came from South America.

BUCKWHEAT   12 inches   *Eriogonum grande* var. *rubescens*

DESCRIPTION: A low woody-based perennial, the short branches tending to lie on the ground with only the tips upright; leaves oblong to egg-shaped, 1-3½ in. long, gray-green with woolly pubescence, the upper leaf surface sometimes without hairs; flower-stalks stout, erect, about 12 in. high, branched at the top, the branches terminated by dense heads of small rose-red flowers.

DISTRIBUTION: *Eriogonum grande* var. *rubescens* occurs on low sandstone cliffs on San Miguel and Santa Rosa Islands and the west end of Santa Cruz Island.

PROPAGATION: By seed which may be planted in flats or in the open ground during late fall or early spring. The seed germinates readily and the seedlings, if grown in flats, can be transplanted to small pots as soon as they are large enough to handle. During the spring months the young plants should be set into the ground where they are to bloom. Once established this species should never be watered during the summer months. This is especially important if the soil tends to be the least bit heavy.

USES: This attractive buckwheat is recommended for rock gardens or for bedding purposes in dry sunny areas. It should not be planted in a mixed border because of the intolerance of the plants to summer watering. Another desirable feature of this species is that it flowers after most of the spring-blooming plants have disappeared and it continues on well into the summer lending color to the garden at a time when it is badly needed.

Little is known about the horticultural history of this plant. It has been grown at both the Santa Barbara Botanic Garden and this Botanic Garden for a number of years.

Another attractive species of Buckwheat is *Eriogonum crocatum* which produces large numbers of bright sulphur yellow flowers in small heads on stalks above the woolly white leaves. *E. crocatum* seldom grows over 6-8 in. tall and it can be used most effectively for edging walks, etc. Cultural recommendations are the same as for the preceding species.

ERIOPHYLLUM *Eriophyllum lanatum* var. *arachnoideum*

10 inches

DESCRIPTION: A low tufted woody-based perennial 6-10 in. tall, stems many from the branching crown; leaves opposite, 1-3 in. long, broadly oval to egg-shaped in outline, the margins of the leaf irregularly and sometimes rather deeply cut into sharp pointed lobes, leaves densely hairy on the under surface, the upper surface green and rather thinly cob-webby, the entire leaf warty in appearance due to the elevation of the leaf tissue between the prominent veins; flower-heads 1-2 in. in diameter, ray-flowers bright yellow, disk-flowers numerous, yellow.

DISTRIBUTION: *Eriophyllum lanatum* var. *arachnoideum* occurs on hillsides at low altitudes from Marin County north to Humboldt County.

PROPAGATION: This species is propagated by seed which germinates readily. The seed can be sown in flats any time from late fall to early spring and the seedlings transplanted when they are large enough to handle. The plants thrive best in a sandy loam with full sun, and in favorable locations they readily volunteer.

USES: This species is recommended for use as a low border along walks, etc. or it can be used for bedding purposes where a low-growing, yellow-flowered perennial is wanted. The plants bloom for long periods of time from late spring well into the summer, a time when few of our natives are at their best. *Eriophyllum lanatum* is a somewhat variable species in nature, but it is believed that the variety *arachnoideum* is the most desirable variety for use in this area. There is little in horticultural history regarding it. *Eriophyllum caespitosum*, a species similar in many ways, and in areas grading into *E. lanatum* var. *arachnoideum*, was introduced into cultivation by David Douglas.

Eriophyllum lanatum var. *arachnoideum*

BEACH STRAWBERRY   8 inches   *Fragaria chiloensis*

DESCRIPTION: A low perennial evergreen 3-8 in. high, plants spreading by means of runners; leaves composed of three separate leaflets, the center one the largest, leaflets 1-1½ in. long, dark glossy green above or dull green in some forms, whitish and covered with hairs on the underside, leaf margins set with 8-10 teeth which are located toward the tip of the leaflets; flowers white, showy, up to 1⅜ in. across, borne in clusters of from 1-6 flowers on stems arising from the crown of the plant; in ours the plants are unisexual, i.e. male and female flowers borne on separate plants; fruit similar to the commercial strawberry, usually small, ½-¾ in. in diameter, edible and of good flavor.

DISTRIBUTION: *Fragaria chiloensis* is found along the coast from San Luis Obispo County north to Alaska. It is also found along the coast of South America from Peru to Patagonia.

PROPAGATION: By runners or by digging older rooted plants.

USES: The Beach Strawberry is especially useful as a ground cover in coastal areas of California, and while it will grow for a distance inland, it should not be planted in the hot interior valleys. Although not particular as to soil, it does best in a rather light sandy loam with good drainage. In coastal areas the plants may be grown in full sun but inland they should be given partial shade. Rooted plants placed about 18 inches apart will produce a solid cover in about six months. Prior to planting the beds should be thoroughly worked

Fragaria chiloensis

and watered to eliminate weeds. The Beach Strawberry must never be put in soil infested with Bermuda Grass as the grass will choke out the strawberries.

After a couple of years the beds will require an annual renovation which consists of a vigorous raking to remove old growth and excess runners. A high mowing of the bed and a light application of a commercial fertilizer should follow. Late winter is probably the best time for this work. While the plants need little water to become established, they grow best if given a light irrigation about once a week during the summer.

The Beach Strawberry varies greatly in leaf size, texture, and length of flowering-stalk, some plants producing the flowers well above the leaves while in others they are almost hidden under the leaves. Different clones also vary in the number of runners produced. In order to insure the production of berries it is necessary to have both staminate and pistillate individuals.

The Hybrid Ornamental Strawberry No. 25 which was produced at this Botanic Garden differs in a number of ways from the Beach Strawberry. The hybrid plants are considerably larger than those of the Beach Strawberry and bear large quantities of dessert-quality fruit. Since these strawberries are perfect-flowered, i.e. both stamens and pistils in the same flower, there is no need for interplanting. This hybrid possesses considerable hybrid vigor and is a very strong grower, so far free from diseases except for a little mildew when grown along the coast and overwatered. It has shown considerable tolerance for heat and can be safely grown in full sun in the intermediate valleys and it has even been reported as doing well in the San Joaquin Valley, but there it should probably have light shade if possible. At the present time this hybrid is being used by some landscape architects as a substitute for Algerian Ivy.

A newer hybrid, No. 41, is similar in all respects except that it produces a somewhat better fruit.

Long before Columbus landed at San Salvador, the Indians of Chile had discovered and used the fruits of the Beach Strawberry, some strains of which produced berries as large as walnuts or even the size of hen's eggs. Plants of the Beach Strawberry were first taken to Europe about 1712. The meadow strawberry, a plant native to eastern United States, had already been introduced into Europe and it is from a cross between the two species that the commercial strawberry that we know today has been developed.

The California Wood Strawberry *(Fragaria californica)* is occasionally grown in gardens. It is not recommended as a ground cover except perhaps for growing on rather shady banks or under trees or shrubbery.

ISLAND ALUM ROOT 12 inches *Heuchera maxima*

DESCRIPTION: A vigorous evergreen perennial arising from a thickened rootstalk, the foliage often forming a rounded clump 12-24 in. across, very old plants may have 1-several stems as much as 1 in. thick and 12 in. long clothed with the clasping bases of living and dead leaves; leaves alternate with a broad clasping base and a petiole 6-10 in. long, leaf blade 4-8 in. across, roundish with 8-10 irregular main lobes, the lobes set with irregular teeth, upper surface of the leaf dark shining green sometimes more or less marbled a lighter color, lower surface light green with hairs on the veins, leaves often turning bright red in age; flowers borne in long narrow clusters 18-30 in. long which often contain several hundred small greenish-white or creamy-white flowers, individual flowers about 3/16 in. long, 5-petaled; fruit a small capsule containing numerous fine black seeds.

DISTRIBUTION: *Heuchera maxima* occurs only on Anacapa, Santa Cruz and Santa Rosa Islands where it is found growing on canyon walls.

57

Heuchera maxima

PROPAGATION: The Island Alum Root is propagated by seeds or by divisions of old plants. Seeds may be planted in the fall or early spring in flats which contain a thin layer of screened sphagnum moss over the soil. After the small seeds are sown on the top of the sphagnum and lightly brushed in, the flat is then moistened by partially immersing it in a pan of water. After being thoroughly soaked, the flat should be covered by a pane of glass to hasten germination. When the seedlings are large enough to handle they should be transplanted to individual containers.

Very recent experiments at this Botanic Garden have shown that growing tips may be broken off old plants and these then rooted in a propagating frame. They can even be placed directly into the ground if the soil is kept moist until they become established. Early spring is probably the best time to produce new plants by this method.

The plants respond best to a shady situation in loamy soil where they may receive water during the summer. After several years they tend to become rangy and unattractive and should be cut back or replaced with young plants.

USES: *Heuchera maxima* is recommended for planting in shady situations in coastal areas and in the intermediate valleys. In addition to the very beautiful mounds of foliage, the plants are attractive during their blooming season, and the light, airy clusters of flowers are excellent for use in floral arrangements.

DOUGLAS IRIS 18 inches *Iris douglasiana*

DESCRIPTION: An evergreen iris often forming clumps several feet in diameter; rhizomes creeping, much smaller than those of the tall bearded varieties, being about ¼-⅜ in. in diameter; leaves sword-like, ½-¾ in. wide and from 1-2 ft. long, dark green with a bright red or purple base; flowering stem with 2-3 leaf-like bracts, often branched, usually 2-3-flowered or as many as 9 flowers on branched stems, flowers composed of 3 petals which in irises are called "standards," and 3 sepals which are called "falls," sepals about 2 in. long and ¾ in. wide, petals about 1¼ in. long and ¾ in. wide, floral parts much larger in improved forms, color variable from deep velvety purple through shades of blue and lavender to white or even yellow; fruit capsule 1½-2½ in. long, triangular in cross section and containing numerous seeds about ⅛ in. in diameter.

DISTRIBUTION: *Iris douglasiana* is found along the coast from Santa Barbara County north to southern Oregon.

PROPAGATION: California irises, of which there are a number of species besides *I. douglasiana*, can be propagated either from seed or by division. A very high percentage of germination (80-95 per cent) can be obtained the first season if a little care is given to the planting of the seed. The seeds should be sown in autumn using a layer of chopped sphagnum moss spread over the top of a regular potting mix. Use of the sphagnum moss greatly reduces the chances of loss from damping-off. The sphagnum should be kept moist and the seed pans placed in a sheltered spot, an unheated greenhouse or cool room being ideal. In about two months the young plants will begin to appear and by the end of January or February most of the seeds will have germinated. When the seedlings are 2 to 3 inches tall they should be transplanted to individual pots and by April they should be large enough to set into the garden. Attention should be given to the plants during the first summer to see that they do not become too dry. The following spring they may be expected to give an abundance of bloom. Especially fine forms can be increased by division. This can be done successfully only when the plants are beginning active growth, either in late fall or early spring. The best way to determine whether they are ready to divide is to dig around the side of the plant with a trowel and if there are heavy white roots an inch or more in length coming from the fans, they are ready. The entire plant can be lifted and the soil washed off the roots with a hose. In this way fewer roots are broken than if the soil is left on and it also makes it possible to see where the divisions should be made. After trimming some of the tops of the leaves, the pieces are ready for replanting. If the material is very important it is best to establish the divisions in pots before again planting in the garden. However, in most instances they can be placed directly into the ground if care is exercised in shading and watering until they are established.

The California irises are not especially particular as to soil type except that they do not thrive under very alkaline conditions. A slightly acid soil containing an abundance of organic material is ideal. The plants should be given almost full sun even in southern California. At the Botanic Garden thousands of these plants are grown on a mesa receiving complete sun all year. In fact, the hot weather of late summer probably helps to insure an abundance of flowers the following season by thoroughly ripening the new growths. It is also our policy to withhold water as much as possible from late July until early September to aid in this ripening process.

Browning of old leaf tips is a natural condition and if this is objectionable they can be trimmed during late fall and winter.

USES: The California irises lend themselves to varied landscaping situations and they are highly recommended for use in coastal areas and intermediate valleys all along the

Iris douglasiana

Pacific Coast from California to Washington. During recent years a number of iris breeders have been concentrating on these plants. Consequently numerous named hybrids are now available on the market. These hybrids vary from plants 6 inches tall and suitable for the rock garden to plants with flower stalks 2 to 3 feet in height. Flower color ranges throughout almost the entire spectrum.

There are a number of other species of iris native to California which are occasionally seen in gardens, but none is as popular as the beautiful little *Iris innominata* which is found in southwestern Oregon. Although not a California species, it would be unfair to gardeners not to mention this most attractive and desirable diminutive plant which has become so very popular not only on the West Coast but also in England, Australia, and New Zealand in a matter of only a few years.

Iris munzii is a vigorous and rank-growing species with blue-green foliage and large flowers ranging in color from lavender to nearly sky-blue. In size this is the largest of all the Pacific Coast irises, and since introduction into cultivation in 1948 is proving to be a most useful one for the plant breeder.

Lobelia cardinalis var. *splendens*

CARDINAL FLOWER 2½ feet *Lobelia cardinalis* var. *splendens*

DESCRIPTION: A perennial herb with simple erect stems 1½-2½ ft. high; leaves narrow near to lance shaped, 3½-5½ in. long, edges irregularly set with fine teeth; flowers borne in a terminal raceme, individual flowers about 1½ in. long, strongly 2-lipped, the upper two lobes of the corolla smaller, erect or recurved, the other 3 lobes pendulous, corolla brilliant and intense red.

DISTRIBUTION: *Lobelia cardinalis* var. *splendens* inhabits moist or boggy areas in the San Gabriel and San Bernardino Mts., south to San Diego County, east to Texas and south to Mexico.

PROPAGATION: With the Cardinal Flower this can be achieved either by division of old plants or by seed. The latter sown in flats germinates in from two weeks to a month and when large enough to handle the seedlings may be transplanted to individual containers and later placed in their permanent locations. Flowers may be expected the first year from fall-sown seed.

USES: *Lobelia cardinalis* var. *splendens* is a most desirable plant for massed groupings in shady moist locations where during the summer and early fall its bright flowers add a most pleasant touch to the shade garden, so often lacking color at that season. However,

61

this species need not be restricted entirely to shady areas, since it can be grown equally well in a sunny spot if the plants are given plenty of water.

The species, of which ours is a variety, has been a garden subject a long while. Apparently it was first introduced into France from seed originally produced in the St. Lawrence Valley and later into England where John Parkinson first mentioned it in 1629. The Cardinal Flower enjoyed a period of great popularity during the Victorian period but today it is seldom seen in cultivation.

YERBA BUENA   6 inches   *Micromeria chamissoni:*

DESCRIPTION: A low trailing evergreen perennial with stems to 2 ft. long; leave pleasantly fragrant, roundish or oval, ½-1 in. long, margins of the leaf set with small rounded teeth, entire plant slightly pubescent, especially the underside of the leaves flowers small, almost white, 2-lipped, borne singly in the axils of the leaves.

DISTRIBUTION: *Micromeria chamissonis* is commonly found in coastal woods from De Norte County south to the Santa Monica Mts. It is also found on Santa Catalina Island.

PROPAGATION: For Yerba Buena the best method of propagation is cuttings which roc readily. Since the creeping stems produce roots where they touch the ground, establishee plants may readily be divided. It is also possible to grow plants from seeds.

PHOTOGRAPH BY DOUGLAS EBERSOLE

Micromeria chamissonis

Uses: Yerba Buena can be used as a ground cover in shady spots such as under trees or it can be allowed to trail over rocks and banks. This plant has long been a favorite of many for the delightful fragrance emitted by the crushed leaves.

Botanically the correct name for this plant is probably *Satureja douglasii.*

SCARLET MONKEY FLOWER   4 feet   *Mimulus cardinalis*

Description: A freely branching perennial herb 2-4 ft. tall, often sprawling; leaves obovate to oblong, 1-3 in. long, strongly 3-nerved, margins set with fine teeth, entire plant pubescent with viscid hairs; flowers borne singly in the axils of the upper leaves, flower 1½-2 in. long, 2-lipped and flattened vertically, the color a brilliant scarlet to orange.

Distribution: *Mimulus cardinalis* is found along stream banks and in seeps on sunny rocky cliffs throughout California, north to southern Oregon, east to Utah and Arizona, and south to Baja California.

Propagation: The Scarlet Monkey Flower is a very tractable plant. Possessing underground rootstocks, old plants are easily divided. This perennial is also grown readily from seed. Being very minute, seeds should be sown thinly in flats. The young seedlings, which appear in a few days, should be transplanted to pots when they are large enough to handle.

Uses: In the garden the Scarlet Monkey Flower appears to flourish in a variety of soil types and in either sun or partial shade. It does best, however, in nearly full sun and in any exposure the plants should be given considerable water. Old plants tend to become rather rank and weedy in appearance, a tendency that can be controlled somewhat by growing them in nearly full sun and by severely pruning them after their period of bloom. Pruning results in new growth and a heavy second flowering. Since the plants bloom the first year from seed they may also be treated as annuals and in many instances are probably best handled in this manner.

Mimulus cardinalis has been grown by gardeners for a long period especially in England where the species was introduced first through seed collected by David Douglas.

PENSTEMON

The genus Penstemon contains a very large number of species, all except one being native of the American continent. They are especially well represented in the flora of California where they occur from the alpine summits of the Sierra Nevada to the hot dry deserts. Indeed the penstemons are among the showiest of all our native plants and between the years 1825 and 1850 many of them were introduced into cultivation, yet today they are not as widely grown as it would seem their beauty would warrant. Percy Everett in his recent account of the California species[1] sums it up well when he says "The truth of the matter is that penstemons are difficult to raise and that a great majority of American gardeners refuse to struggle for years to succeed with a slow and perverse plant."

Today however, interest in growing these beautiful plants is increasing as more gardeners succeed in learning how to correctly handle them. To that end a national penstemon society has been formed, an organization all serious penstemon enthusiasts should join. Through their bulletin the gardener can learn much about this interesting group.

The species recommended here (and under shrubs) are chosen because they are very showy and are somewhat easier to grow than many of the others. For a more complete discussion of the California penstemons the reader is referred to Everett's excellent account of them.

[1]Percy C. Everett. *The California Penstemons.* El Aliso 2: 155-198, 1950.

PENSTEMON   2 feet   *Penstemon heterophyllus* var. *australis*

DESCRIPTION: A perennial 9-24 in. tall, much-branched from the base forming rounded clumps to 3 ft. in diameter, branches ascending; leaves opposite, narrow, linear to lance-shaped, the upper reduced, entire plant minutely hairy; flowers borne along the upper portions of the stem producing a long narrow spike-like inflorescence, flowers tubular and 2-lipped, 1-1¼ in. long, blue to lavender and purple.

DISTRIBUTION: *Penstemon heterophyllus* var. *australis* occurs in the chaparral belt from Monterey County south to San Diego County.

PROPAGATION: This species is propagated by seed which germinates readily. It may be planted in flats during the fall and the young seedlings when about an inch high moved to individual containers or it may be sown directly in the open ground where the plants are desired. Plants grown from fall-sown seed will bloom the first summer.

In the garden they should be given a dry sunny spot in a coarse well-drained soil, however if not watered during the summer months this species will perform well for a year or so in heavy soil. Even in nature *Penstemon heterophyllus* var. *australis* is probably rather short-lived so it is best to plan to replace it about every second or third year. This, however, becomes unnecessary in many instances because of the numerous seedlings which spring up around the old plants.

Penstemon heterophyllus var. *australis*

USES: This penstemon is recommended very highly to gardeners in southern California. Indeed there are few natives which will produce such an abundance of color in the garden for such a long period of time. The one objection might be that some forms of this species tend to be an unattractive shade of magenta. However, since the color varies considerably from one plant to another, it is often possible to obtain a strain with a more desirable flower color by saving seed from selected plants. At least two horticultural varieties of this species are on the market, 'California Blue Bedder' and 'Blue Gem'. Both are supposed to have the rarest of all colors in flowers, a bright and intense true blue.

Penstemon heterophyllus has been in cultivation a long while, having been discovered by Douglas and introduced into horticulture in 1834.

Pestemon spectabilis

PENSTEMON   5 feet   *Penstemon spectabilis*

DESCRIPTION: A large erect perennial as much as 5 ft. in height and often equally broad; leaves opposite, the lower ones with a petiole and a leaf blade 3-4 in. long, ovate to oblanceolate, coarsely but irregularly toothed, upper leaves smaller and the bases united around the stem; inflorescence a large open, much-branched panicle 1-1½ ft. long bearing up to several hundred flowers; flowers 2-lipped, 1-1½ in. long, broadly funnelform, variable in color but usually lavender-purple often with blue corolla lobes, pinkish in the bud.

DISTRIBUTION: *Penstemon spectabilis* is found in dry washes and on rocky open hillsides from Los Angeles County south to Baja California.

PROPAGATION: Seed sown in flats during the fall or early spring germinates in from 2 to 4 weeks and the young plants can be potted in about two months. In the garden the plants should be given a rather sterile, sandy or coarse, well-drained soil with full sun and very little water during the summer. They can even be grown in heavy loam if they are not watered during the summer. Since the plants by nature are probably rather short-lived, gardeners should plan to replace them every few years. In favorable areas this will be unnecessary since new ones volunteer very readily.

USES: *Penstemon spectabilis* is considered to be the most showy of all our native penstemons and a mass of it in flower is a memorable sight. This Beard Tongue is highly recommended for larger gardens where its cultural requirements can be met.

Introduction into cultivation was in England by Messrs. Low, of Clapton in 1861.

Other species which are considered to be of value for southern California are *Penstemon centranthifolius,* the familiar Scarlet Bugler, with its long narrow flowers of bright scarlet, *P. eatonii* which is in many ways similar to *centranthifolius* with the exceptions of slightly more funnelform flowers and flower stalks that tend to stand more upright than in *centranthifolius. P. palmeri* has tall stalks of large, usually pale lavender-pink flowers, notable for their fragrance.

BLUE-EYED GRASS   18 inches   *Sisyrinchium bellum*

DESCRIPTION: An herbaceous perennial with narrow grass-like leaves and flattened stems 10-18 in. high, stems branched with 3-7 flowers at their tips, flowers saucer-shaped, about ¾ in. in diameter, composed of 6 blue or purple perianth segments, each with a conspicuous yellow spot at the base; seed capsules globose, containing numerous black seeds.

DISTRIBUTION: *Sisyrinchium bellum* is found on moist grassy slopes throughout much of California although it is rare in the desert and the arid regions east of the Sierras.

PROPAGATION: Blue-eyed Grass is very easily propagated either by dividing old plants or by seed which may be sown directly in the ground where the plants are wanted or sown in flats, later moving the young seedlings to their permanent locations.

USES: Thriving in nearly any soil, either in full sun or partial shade, Blue-eyed Grass is easily grown. The small flowers, borne in abundance from March through May, vary considerably in color from pure white (which is rare), to pale blue, blue and dark purple. The flowers open only in sunlight and last but a single day, however they are produced in such large numbers that a planting may appear to be nearly a solid sheet of color for long periods during the spring months. Blue-eyed Grass can be used as a bedding plant but it is more desirable for filling in areas around plantings of shrubs and trees.

Sisyrinchium californicum is an attractive yellow-flowered species which in other respects is similar to *S. bellum.*

66

Sisyrinchium bellum

CALIFORNIA FUCHSIA   18 inches   *Zauschneria californica*

DESCRIPTION: A low herbaceous perennial forming rounded mats to 18 in. across, lower branches becoming somewhat woody in age; leaves alternate, variable, green or grayish, linear to broadly lance-shaped, entire plant hairy and glandular; flowers borne in terminal spikes, flowers large, fuchsia-like, brilliant scarlet, tube inflated just above the ovary then becoming funnel-form, calyx-lobes 4, petals 4; seed capsules linear, erect and often curved, seeds with a tuft of hairs at one end.

DISTRIBUTION: *Zauschneria californica* inhabits the valleys and foothills from Sonoma and Lake counties southward through the inner and outer Coast Ranges to coastal southern California and northern Baja California, rarely is it found in the low foothills of the Sierra Nevadas.

PROPAGATION: The California Fuchsia is propagated mainly by readily-germinated seeds, but it can be grown from cuttings or by divisions of old plants. Because plants spread underground, in some cultivated areas it has become obnoxious. If the seed is sown in flats the young plants should be transplanted to small containers when large enough to handle and then later moved to their permanent locations. In the garden they should be given a

67

site with a light soil and full sun, although the plants will do fairly well in heavy soil if they are given very little water during the summer.

This species is extremely variable in nature both in leaf shape and size as well as in plant habit. The flowers, however, do not vary a great deal and the color is remarkably constant throughout the genus with the exception of an albino form which is occasionally grown.

USES: This California native is notable for producing masses of brilliant color during late summer and continuing well into the fall—a season when few California natives are at their best. Consequently it is highly recommended for bedding purposes in dry sunny locations or for covering dry slopes. It can also be used in the rock garden. Due to the tendency of the plants to become leggy it is best to place them fairly close together and to pinch back the young shoots until a compact well-branched individual is developed.

The California Fuchsia has been known to gardeners for a long while, having been apparently first collected by Haenke at Monterey in 1791. It was not, however, grown in cultivation until sometime later. In 1845, when the Horticultural Society of London decided to send a man to collect for them in California, *Zauschneria californica* was one of the plants they were most eager to receive and they wrote, "We trust that it will not disappoint the expectations that we have formed of it." Later when Lindley was writing about the species he said, "This curious plant, which it has long been an object to obtain, proves to be a species of much horticultural interest."

Zauschneria californica

3. Shrubs

CALIFORNIA COPPERLEAF — 3 feet — *Acalypha californica*

DESCRIPTION: A small rigidly branched evergreen shrub 1-3 ft. tall; leaves alternate, broadly ovate, ½-1¼ in. long, edges set with fine rounded teeth, leaves glandular pubescent, deep green above, prominently veined on the under side; flowers small, inconspicuous, staminate and pistillate flowers borne separately but on the same plant, staminate flowers in small catkin-like clusters, ½-1¼ in. long, pistillate flowers in small clusters of from one to several flowers borne at the base of the staminate spike, corolla absent, calyx 3-8-lobed; fruit a 3-celled capsule often surrounded by an enlarged bract.

FLOWERING: April and May in the wild but nearly all year when grown in cultivation.

Acalypha californica

DISTRIBUTION: *Acalypha californica* is found occasionally on dry hills in southern San Diego County and south into Mexico.

PROPAGATION: The California Copperleaf is propagated either by cuttings or by seed. At the Rancho Santa Ana Botanic Garden the best results have been obtained from seed which, sown in flats in the late fall, germinates within a few weeks. The young plants can be potted when large enough to handle and planted later into their permanent locations. In the garden this species should be given a light, well-drained soil in either full sun or partial shade. If given a small amount of water during the summer months the plants remain more attractive than they otherwise would.

USES: This rather rare and little-known California shrub can be used for hedges or as a low filler plant. It stands clipping well and when used as a hedge it can be kept low. There is, however, one thing that must be taken into consideration in using this plant and that is that it is injured by temperatures much below 28°F. Its use, therefore, is restricted to nearly frost-free areas.

Nothing is known as to the horticultural history of this species. It has been grown at the Botanic Garden since 1939.

RED SHANKS   20 feet   *Adenostoma sparsifolium*

DESCRIPTION: A shrub or small tree 6-20 ft. tall with yellowish-green bark becoming red in age and peeling off in thin sheets; leaves heather-like, evergreen, scattered and alternate, linear, ¼-¾ in. long, glandular dotted; flowers borne in loose clusters ¾-2½ in. long, white or rarely pinkish, fragrant, individual flowers small, about 1/16 in. in diameter.

FLOWERING: July and August.

DISTRIBUTION: *Adenostoma sparsifolium* occurs in the chaparral between 2000-6000 feet altitude from Santa Barbara County south to San Diego County and western Imperial County.

PROPAGATION: Red Shanks is propagated by seed, or, according to Rehder, by green-wood cuttings taken in the spring. Seed germination may be poor and it has been suggested by Mirov and Kraebel that the seeds be treated with 10% sulphuric acid for 15 minutes and then planted. The young seedlings can be moved to individual containers when they are large enough to handle and later planted in the garden.

This species should be given a sunny location in coarse, dry soil. The plants may be watered during the summer although it is unnecessary after they are once established.

USES: Red Shanks is recommended only for large native gardens where it can be used effectively as a tall background plant. The foliage is delightfully fragrant especially after rains.

According to Rehder, *Adenostoma sparsifolium* was introduced into cultivation in 1891.

Another species is *Adenostoma fasciculatum*, the familiar Chamise of the chaparral areas, which differs from *A. sparsifolium* mainly in having the leaves in fascicles instead of scattered and in the old bark being gray, or very dark, rather than reddish. The plants are in general smaller than those of *A. sparsifolium*. *A. fasciculatum* is very common in the chaparral and is the dominant shrub in such areas. Propagation and handling is the same as for *A. sparsifolium*.

Adenostoma fasciculatum

71

SHAW'S AGAVE   3 feet (10 feet when in flower)   *Agave shawii*

DESCRIPTION: A large fleshy succulent with a short trunk clothed with old leaves; leaves 8-20 in. long and 3-5 in. wide, lance-ovate, broadest above the middle, green, glossy, tip of leaf set with a large sharp spine and the edges of the leaf set with large,

Agave shawii

hooked, garnet-red prickles; inflorescence as much as 10 ft. tall, branched near the top, flower-stalk covered with leafy, appressed bracts with spiny tips; flowers numerous, 2½-3½ in. long, greenish-yellow, in compact clusters of from 20-30 flowers, each filled with a sweetish nectar.

FLOWERING: December to March.

DISTRIBUTION: *Agave shawii* is probably extinct at the present time in California but formerly it was common along the coast of San Diego County from Pt. Loma south to the border. It occurs in abundance along the coast of northern Baja California.

PROPAGATION: *Agave shawii* is propagated by seeds which germinate readily, or by suckers removed from the base of old plants. Young seedlings when growing in flats should be watered very carefully to prevent them from damping-off. When large enough to handle they may be potted into individual containers and within a year they will usually be large enough to move to the garden. A faster means of propagation is to remove the offshoots from the old plants. The lower leaves should be removed and the offshoot then planted where it is wanted. The ground should be kept fairly dry to prevent rotting. *Agave shawii* will grow in practically any soil except one that is strongly alkaline, however, it grows most rapidly when given a light sandy well-drained loam. It should, of course, have full sun.

USES: This succulent is one of the finest native to California and is highly recommended for gardens. It is also most useful for covering sunny banks and slopes, since it spreads and will, within a few years, produce large clumps. The tall, striking flower-stalks appear during late fall and the flowers open during mid-winter, a time when few other natives are blooming. After flowering the old plant dies but is replaced by numerous suckers which appear around the base of the old clump.

Because of the very sharp and dangerous spines on the leaves, the plants should not be grown where small children might be hurt by them.

According to the German publication "Gartenflora" *Agave shawii* was first discovered in 1850 by Dr. Parker who apparently sent seeds of it to the famous German nursery firm of Haage and Schmidt who first grew it.

ISLAND MANZANITA   8 feet   *Arctostaphylos insularis*

DESCRIPTION: A spreading evergreen shrub as much as 8 ft. tall, with dark red bark, young branches glandular-hairy, greenish; leaves alternate, oblong-ovate to ovate, or elliptical, bright green and glossy above, 1-2 in. long, leathery, oriented so that the blades are nearly vertical; flowers borne in rather large spreading clusters at the tips of the branches, individual flowers urn-shaped, white, fragrant, about ½ in. long; fruit yellowish-brown, smooth, about ⅜ in. thick.

FLOWERING: January to March.

DISTRIBUTION: *Arctostaphylos insularis* occurs on dry rocky slopes at 10-1000 ft. altitude on Santa Cruz, Santa Rosa and Santa Catalina Islands.

PROPAGATION: The Island Manzanita is propagated either by cuttings or by seed which is slow to germinate. According to Mirov, species of Arctostaphylos usually require treatment of seed with sulphuric acid followed by prolonged stratification in order to obtain good germination. The same author also says that they are easily propagated by cuttings, especially when treated with root-inducing substances.

If grown from seed the young plants should be transferred to individual containers when large enough to handle and planted into their permanent locations later. In the garden they should, if possible, be given a heavy rocky soil in a sunny location with moderate watering during the summer months.

In recent years a disease has caused great losses among species of Arctostaphylos both in nature as well as in garden plantings. According to Clark of the University of California at Los Angeles, who made a survey of the plantings at the Rancho Santa Ana Botanic Garden in 1948, the first symptoms of the disease, which is caused by a fungus called *Botryosphaeria,* is the presence of occasional blighted twigs and branches. The leaves on infected limbs turn brown and become dry but do not drop off immediately. On older branches cankers may be found. The disease, however, is slow in killing the plants and an infected individual may remain alive for several years. So far a control has not been discovered. From Clark's investigation it would appear that overhead watering causes a rapid spread of the disease and consequently this type of irrigation should not be used. Of the species of Manzanita grown at the Botanic Garden, *Arctostaphylos insularis* was the least often affected with the fungus and no loss has occurred due to this disease.

USES: This species is most effective as an accent or background plant and it is very beautiful when in flower. It is also one of the native shrubs which is interesting all year, its leaves remaining attractive even through the summer when many of the native plants become partially bare.

Nothing is known about the horticultural history of this shrub.

Arctostaphylos insularis

Atriplex hymenelytra

DESERT HOLLY   3 feet   *Atriplex hymenelytra*

DESCRIPTION: A small, erect, compactly branched, evergreen shrub 1-3 ft. tall, herbage silvery-white; leaves alternate, numerous, ½-1¼ in. long, roundish or ovate, the margins wavy and deeply and irregularly toothed so that the entire leaf presents a very holly-like appearance; flowers borne in small clusters, the staminate and pistillate flowers on separate plants, individual flowers small, inconspicuous, pistillate plants covered with reddish fruits during the fall.

FLOWERING: February to April.

DISTRIBUTION: *Atriplex hymenelytra* is found on dry alkaline slopes and flats in the Colorado and Mojave deserts, east to Utah and south to Mexico.

PROPAGATION: The Desert Holly is propagated by seeds which should be sown in flats containing a coarse sandy loam or other porous mixture. Germination takes place in a couple of weeks and the young seedlings can be transplanted to individual containers when they are large enough to handle. If possible, in the garden the plants should be given a light sandy soil, although they can be grown in nearly any soil except heavy clay. The plants need full sun and they will tolerate a small amount of water during the summer months. At the Rancho Santa Ana Botanic Garden they have done well but they tend to be short-lived.

USES: Desert Holly is certainly one of the best known of the native plants both here and in other sections of the United States where it is shipped for holiday decoration. Unfortunately it is a shrub which cannot be recommended to most gardeners. For those living in desert regions such as around Palm Springs, or in hot dry interior areas where its cultural requirements can be met, it makes a most attractive small shrub which is at its best during the winter months. Warning should be given that this species is especially relished by rabbits.

In recent years Desert Holly has become rare in some localities due to heavy harvesting for the florists' trade and it is now protected by law with heavy penalties being inflicted on anyone collecting plants on public-owned land.

Regarding its history in horticulture, nothing is known.

PROSTRATE COYOTE BRUSH

2 feet *Baccharis pilularis* var. *pilularis*

DESCRIPTION: A low evergreen shrub forming a mat 6-24 in. high and as much as 6-15 ft. across; branches flexible, seldom over ¾ in. in diameter, occasionally rooting where they touch the ground; leaves alternate, dark green to gray-green, ½-¾ in. long, egg-shaped to broadly oval, usually with about 5 coarse teeth; flowers of two kinds and produced on separate plants, pistillate flowers borne in small heads of 20-50 flowers, similar to other members of the Sunflower Family except that the flower-heads have no rays, staminate flowers borne in similar heads; achenes (seeds) with a small crown of shiny white down which allows them to be distributed by the wind.

FLOWERING: September and October.

DISTRIBUTION: *Baccharis pilularis* var. *pilularis* inhabits exposed and usually wind-swept sand dunes and bluffs along the coast from the Russian River in Sonoma County south to Pt. Sur in Monterey County, extending inland only about as far as Berkeley.

PROPAGATION: The Prostrate Coyote Brush may be grown either from seeds or cuttings. Seed sown in flats or outdoor seed-beds in late fall or winter will germinate within a few weeks. When the young seedlings are large enough to handle, they may be transplanted to individual containers and a short time later set into their permanent locations. Cuttings may be rooted almost every month of the year, but summer cuttings should be taken only if cool temperatures can be provided in the propagating frames.

USES: Prostrate Coyote Brush has proven to be a most desirable ground cover at the Rancho Santa Ana Botanic Garden where it does well in full sun and in heavy loam. Here it forms a low mat about 12-18 in. high which is attractive the entire year. This species also does well in shade or semishade, but it should not be planted under trees which drop foliage, particularly large leaves, constantly, since the fallen leaves are difficult to remove from the Baccharis. This species is also valuable for planting on banks, cuts, etc.

While the plants will grow with no summer watering, it is recommended that they be irrigated about once a month if possible. Young plantings should be rolled and all upright branches removed as soon as they appear.

There are two very important things to be considered in using this shrub as a ground cover. Since the pistillate plants produce considerable seed which is shed during the fall, they are not as attractive as the staminate. For that reason it is recommended that only male or staminate plants be used. Another factor to keep in mind is the variation occurring in seed-grown plants. Individuals from one lot of seed may differ in leaf color and size as well as in plant form some being much more prostrate than others. Too, individuals grown from seed will consist of both male and female forms. However the seedlings may be placed fairly close together and the pistillate removed when they bloom.

For best results from the use of this species as a ground cover it is recommended that all the plants set into an area be propagated by cuttings from a single staminate individual and that this plant be carefully chosen for height and desirable leaf characters. In this way a very high degree of uniformity will be achieved, a feature especially important in shrubs used as ground covers.

It is believed that Prostrate Coyote Brush is one of the most desirable of our natives for use as a medium low ground cover in southern California.

This species has been grown at the Rancho Santa Ana Botanic Garden since 1930.

Baccharis pilularis var. *pilularis*

CHUPAROSA   4 feet   *Beloperone californica*

DESCRIPTION: A low spreading intricately-branched shrub 2-4 ft. high with slender dull green branches; leaves opposite, small, ovate to round, ¼-¾ in. long, soon deciduous; flowers in dense clusters at the ends of the branches, dull red in color, tubular, 2-lipped, 1-1½ in. long.

FLOWERING: February to April but in cultivation some flowers may be found almost throughout the entire year.

DISTRIBUTION: *Beloperone californica* occurs on the western and northern edges of the Colorado Desert where it is found along water courses at altitudes below 2500 feet. It is also found in Baja California.

PROPAGATION: Chuparosa is propagated by readily-germinated seeds and the young plants should be transplanted to individual containers when they are large enough to handle. In the garden the plants should be given a well-drained soil and a sunny location. This species responds well to some summer watering, and if severely pruned each year it will produce a well-rounded shrub which will bloom freely.

USES: Chuparosa has not been widely used as an ornamental in the state and is seldom seen in gardens. It is, however, an interesting subject which responds well to cultivation; and because of its winter-blooming habit when the plants are leafless and when few other natives are in flower, it could be used to advantage in native gardens in the warmer parts of the state.

OREGON GRAPE   3 feet   *Berberis aquifolium*

DESCRIPTION: An erect freely branching evergreen shrub 3-5 ft. tall; leaves 4-10 in. long, composed of a terminal leaflet with 4-8 leaflets arranged in pairs along the axis of the leaf, leaflets 1-2½ in. long, ¾-1½ in. broad, rather thin and leathery, glossy dark green above, leaf margins set with sharp spines, the leaflets very holly-like; flowers small, yellow, borne in dense clusters; fruit a black berry about ¼ in. in diameter covered with a waxy violet bloom.

FLOWERING: February to March.

DISTRIBUTION: *Berberis aquifolium* (also known as *Mahonia aquifolium*) is found in wooded mountain regions from British Columbia south to Trinity and Humboldt counties in northern California.

PROPAGATION: Oregon Grape is propagated from seeds, suckers, or layering. Seeds may be sown soon after harvest in flats or in outdoor seed beds. When the seedlings are about 1 in. high they should be transplanted to pots and later to gallon cans. Soils or locations are not critical and the species will grow even in heavy clay. They should be given water during the summer and in the interior valleys they should have considerable shade. The plants spread by underground suckers, are free from diseases and the only insect pest which sometimes bothers them is leaf-miner.

USES: Oregon Grape is very highly recommended for garden planting in California and it can be used as a hedge, for foundation planting, as a filler, or for mass planting. The plants require little pruning except to keep them from becoming leggy. There is a lower growing form of this species on the market called *B. aquifolium* var. *compacta* which is useful when a somewhat smaller plant is required.

Berberis aquifolium was first introduced into cultivation from seed collected by Lewis and Clark on their expedition to the Pacific Northwest in 1804-1806. Later Douglas introduced it into England from plants which he obtained from a nursery in New York in 1823. There, it is said, this species caused a sensation and large sums were paid for the plants. The Oregon Grape thrives in areas along the Atlantic seaboard and it is probably the most popular of the native West Coast shrubs grown in the East.

Berberis aquilfolium

Berberis nevinii

NEVIN'S BARBERRY   10 feet   *Berberis nevinii*

DESCRIPTION: A much-branched evergreen shrub 3-10 ft. tall; leaves alternate, but often congested into small clusters, gray-green (young ones reddish), hard, each leaf composed of 3-5, or even 7, leaflets arranged with one terminal with the others set opposite each other, leaflets narrow oblong, pointed, terminal ones 1-1½ in. long, lateral ones ¾-1 in. long, leaf margins set with sharp bristles; flowers borne in short, loose 5-9-flowered clusters at the end of the short spur branches, individual flowers small, about ¼ in. in diameter, yellow, usually with 6 petals; fruit a more or less translucent yellowish-red berry.

FLOWERING: March-May.

DISTRIBUTION: *Berberis nevinii* (also known as *Mahonia nevinii*) is a very local species found only in a few places in Los Angeles, San Bernardino, Riverside, and San Diego counties.

PROPAGATION: Seed of this barberry should be planted in the fall in outdoor seed beds or in flats. Germination will usually take place the following spring. When the seedlings are about an inch high they should be transplanted to individual containers and they will then be ready to set out that fall. The stem tips should be pinched early in order to induce the plant to branch. This barberry is not particular as to soil and does well even in heavy adobe. It can also stand more summer watering than can most natives and will either take drought or ordinary garden care.

USES: Nevin's Barberry is recommended highly for planting in southern California. It can be used successfully as a specimen plant, as an evergreen filler, for foundation planting, or as an unclipped hedge. It is attractive during March and April when it is in bloom, again during June and July when the fruits are ripe, and the foliage is neat and of a desirable quality all during the year.

Berberis nevinii was first collected in 1882 by Rev. Nevin of Los Angeles and it was introduced into cultivation by Theodore Payne, who first grew it about thirty years ago.

Berberis nevinii fruit

Berberis nevinii flowers

SPICE BUSH   9 feet   *Calycanthus occidentalis*

DESCRIPTION: An erect widely spreading deciduous shrub 4-9 ft. tall; leaves opposite, egg-shaped to broadly lance-shaped, 2-6 in. long, tapering to a point, dark green, surface of the leaf harsh to the touch, fragrant when bruised, flowers 1½-2½ in. in diameter, borne singly at the ends of the branches, petals many, narrow and curved, about 1 in. long, dull reddish-brown on the outside, the upper part of the petal brown in age; fruit a woody urn-shaped receptacle about 1 in. long containing numerous seeds.

DISTRIBUTION: *Calycanthus occidentalis* is found along streams and on moist canyon slopes in the Coast Ranges from Sonoma and Napa counties north to Trinity County and in the Sierra Nevada foothills from Shasta County to Tulare County.

PROPAGATION: The Spice Bush may be grown from seeds, cuttings or by dividing old plants. Seeds sown in flats germinate in about a month and the seedlings may be transplanted to individual containers when they are large enough to handle. This species has not been propagated by cuttings at the Rancho Santa Ana Botanic Garden but it is reported that they root easily.

USES: This shrub does well in shady, moist or wet places and is very useful for background and naturalistic plantings along water courses, etc. The large glossy leaves are most attractive and the flowers are very different from those found on any other California plant.

This Spice Bush was first introduced into cultivation in 1831 from seed collected by Douglas.

Calycanthus occidentalis

Calycanthus occidentalis

83

TREE ANEMONE   15 feet   *Carpenteria californica*

DESCRIPTION: An erect evergreen shrub 6-15 ft. tall, branching from near the base to form a dense bush, older stems with light tan, shedding bark; leaves opposite, oblong and tapering at either end, rather thick, deep green, 3-5 in. long and about half as wide, margins of leaf tending to roll under, upper surface of leaf smooth, lower surface covered with a mat of white hairs; flowers borne in terminal clusters of from 3-12 flowers, individual flowers large, 2-3 in. in diameter, white, composed of from 5-6 or even 8 petals with a conspicuous yellow center made up of a cluster of stamens; fruit a conical capsule ⅜-½ in. in diameter containing many small seeds.

FLOWERING: May to August, but under cultivation the plants may produce flowers during other months.

DISTRIBUTION: *Carpenteria californica* is a very local species known from only a few localities in the foothills of the Sierra Nevada between the San Joaquin River and the Kings River where it grows at altitudes of from 2000-3000 feet.

PROPAGATION: Carpenteria can be propagated by cuttings, suckers, or seed. The tiny seeds are best sown in a thin layer of screened sphagnum placed over the regular soil mix. After careful watering a pane of glass should be put over the flat to hasten germination. The seedlings, small and delicate at first, should be transplanted when they are large enough to handle into a gritty well-drained soil mixture. Great care should be taken not to overwater them since they are very susceptible to damping-off.

The plants are best held in the lath house the first season and set into their permanent locations during the following fall or winter, early enough, however, so they become established before summer. In the garden they should be given a well-drained soil and partial shade with very little or no water during the summer months once they are established.

Carpenteria is often affected by a leaf-curl which makes the plants unsightly. This is caused by attacks of aphids and can be controlled by spraying the plants as soon as the leaf-curl is detected.

USES: Carpenteria is one of the finest of all our native shrubs and is invariably included in any list of the ten best native shrubs of the state. It was first discovered by General Fremont on one of his expeditions through the interior of the state during the years 1843 to 1848. His rather poor specimen was known to have come from the Sierras but the exact locality was unknown and for many years Carpenteria was a "lost" species.

In 1875 Dr. Gustav Eisen of the Fancher Creek Nurseries of Fresno rediscovered it in Fresno County on Big Dry Creek northeast of Fresno where he found a colony of approximately one thousand plants. Dr. Eisen collected 25 pounds of fruit which he sent to a florist in Washington, D. C. who in turn distributed the seed to other florists in eastern United States and Europe.

Flowering specimens were first exhibited in California at a meeting of the California Academy of Science in San Francisco on September 4, 1876. Carpenteria has been offered for sale by nurserymen in California at least since 1908.

There is some variation between plants of Carpenteria and exceptionally fine forms should be propagated by cuttings. In England there is a named variety which has flowers as much as 3½ in. in diameter.

Carpenteria californica

CEANOTHUS

Of the many shrubs native to California, the genus Ceanothus contains more species which are of interest, or importance, to gardeners than any other single genus. Included in the group, which is often referred to as the California Lilacs, although they are in no way related to the true lilac, are plants which vary all the way from prostrate ground covers and small shrubs to small trees, and in flower color from pure white through shades of blue and lavender to deep blue and purple, occasionally pure pink. While some species are deciduous, those found in California are all evergreen, or at the most, only partially deciduous.

Many of the native species were introduced into Europe about the middle of the last century and most of them have been grown in cultivation either in Europe or in California. In recent years interest in this group has developed to the point where now nearly all the larger nurseries in the state handle at least a few of the native species.

In 1942 Maunsell Van Rensselaer, formerly of the Santa Barbara Botanic Garden, and H. E. McMinn, of Mills College, published a comprehensive and well-illustrated book devoted to this group[1]. In their work there is a section covering what is known concerning propagation and recommendations for growing the various species in the garden as well as botanical descriptions of all known species. This very excellent account of the Ceanothi should be consulted by all gardeners who are interested in growing these shrubs in their gardens.

As Walter E. Lammerts recently pointed out (Jour. Calif. Hort. Soc. 9: 121-125, 1948) in spite of the enthusiasm which gardeners have shown for these native shrubs in recent years it must be admitted that many of them have rather serious faults which restrict their use in the garden.

Probably the most serious single fault is the fact that most of the native species cannot tolerate water during the summer months and therefore cannot be placed in mixed plantings with shrubs and trees which require irrigation during that time. This is especially true of the very beautiful San Diego Lilac *(Ceanothus cyaneus)* which has in the past few years become quite popular with gardeners in southern California.

The first Ceanothus to be grown in cultivation was the white-flowered *Ceanothus americanus,* a native of eastern and central United States which was introduced into Europe in 1713. During the first or second decade of the nineteenth century a blue-flowered species, *C. coeruleus,* was introduced into France from Mexico. From crosses between these two species there have been developed a number of horticultural varieties which are adapted to continental conditions and which are held in high esteem by gardeners both on the Continent and in England. Probably the best known of the French hybrids is the very lovely 'Gloire de Versailles.' Unfortunately none of these European varieties do well in southern California although they can be grown successfully from the San Francisco Bay area north to British Columbia. The important point, however, is that by interspecific hybridization the Europeans were able to combine the desirable color of *C. coeruleus,* which is in some respects similar to *C. cyaneus,* with the hardiness and ability to stand summer watering of *C. americanus.*

Beginning with the pioneer work of Lammerts in 1941 several plant breeders have commenced working on the hybridization of the California species with the view in mind of producing varieties which are more amenable to garden conditions than are the native species, while at the same time producing shrubs which have good leaf characteristics, desirable flower color, and good plant habit.

Since 1948 the Rancho Santa Ana Botanic Garden has maintained a test plot, first in

---

[1]Maunsell Van Rensselaer and Howard E. McMinn. *Ceanothus,* 308 pp. 1942. Santa Barbara Botanic Garden, Santa Barbara, California.

Orange County and later at Claremont in Los Angeles County, where the various named hybrids have been grown under uniform conditions. The observations reported here were made from these plants. In all cases the plants have been allowed to develop normally in order to ascertain how large they will grow and what form they will take without pruning.

'Sierra Blue': This clone and the one following were selected by Walter Lammerts and released to the trade in 1948. It was selected from seedlings of 'La Primavera' which in turn was raised from seed collected from *C. cyaneus*. The influence of that species is very evident in this clone. Our plants are now 12-15 feet tall and wider at the top than at the bottom. Leaves are relatively sparse and the entire plant has a very open and lanky appearance. Branching is irregular and there is no gracefulness about the plant. The inflorescences are quite large and the color is very good being a deep blue-purple. Indeed, when the plants are in bloom they have very much the same appearance as *cyaneus* itself, and as in that species, it too, is very late in coming into flower. This variety is certainly not to be recommended for planting where there is not considerable space available. In any case, it should be situated in the background with lower growing shrubs around the base so that the plants will not appear so leggy. Judicious pruning when the plants are young should also help.

'Mountain Haze': As mentioned above, this clone came from the same lot of seedlings as 'Sierra Blue'. It is, however, a very different plant. In Orange County the plants grew to a height of about 5 feet and they were nearly as broad. The leaves were abundant, well distributed and of a dark green color. The flowers were borne in medium-sized clusters and were a dark clear blue. In form this clone is superior to 'Sierra Blue' but from our experience it would appear that it was a shy bloomer. It has not been grown at the Claremont site and under different environmental conditions it might bloom more abundantly.

'Blue Cloud': The Botanic Garden specimens are now about 8 feet tall and from 8-10 feet across. In form they are rounded and compact. The leaves are relatively small, well distributed and abundant. The inflorescences are quite small and in color the flowers are a pale gray-blue. In plant form this variety is certainly one of the finest and would be most useful as a screening plant if sufficient room is available for it. It is branched to the ground and would not only be a barrier to children but it is dense enough to be an effective low windbreak.

'Royal Blue': Our plants are now 4-5 feet tall and up to 10 feet across with the tips of the longer branches lying on the ground. The leaves being medium in size and only fairly abundant cause the plant to be somewhat open in appearance. The inflorescences are medium sized and the flower color is a very intense blue-purple. The strongest criticism of this clone is that the plants have the appearance of being broken, as though weighted down by snow, or having been run over when they were young. This feature might be used to advantage if they were grown at the top of a bank where they would be viewed from below. Otherwise it is doubtful whether this variety should be grown by the average gardener.

'Mary Lake': Plants 4-5 feet tall and about 8 feet across. In form this variety is quite a bit like the preceding one. It does, however, have the advantage of having better leaf characters. Not only is the leaf color better but the leaves are smaller and more numerous making the plant not quite so open in appearance. The flower clusters are medium sized and of a dark blue color.

'Blue Sky': Our plants are 6-8 feet tall and 8-10 feet broad. They are symmetrical and the form is quite good. The leaves are larger than in the clones previously described and they are only fairly abundant. The crowning glory of this variety is its flowers. The inflorescences are large and rather open and the flowers are a very beautiful almost sky-blue color. When in flower this is undoubtedly the finest of all the clones. It is probably best used as a specimen plant.

'Julia Phelps': Plants 5-6 feet tall and 6 feet across. In form this variety is relatively compact and well branched, the leaves are quite small (about ½ in. long and ¼ in. wide), they are abundant and well distributed. The inflorescences are small and nearly globose in shape with deep cobalt-blue flowers. Visually this clone is quite distinct from the others so far described.

'Mills Glory': This hybrid is the result of a cross between *C. purpureus* and *C. gloriosus,* two species belonging to the section *Cerastes* of the genus, whereas those described earlier are all hybrids between species of the *Euceanothus* section. At Claremont this hybrid has grown to a height of about 2½ ft. with a spread of 7-8 ft. In form it is compact and so far has produced no strong-growing upright leaders. The leaves are most pleasing in appearance, being dark green and shiny and very holly-like. They are abundant and well spaced on the plant. While the flowers are attractive, this useful hybrid should be grown for the desirable habit rather than just for the bloom.

'Apple Blossom': This is a selection made here at the Botanic Garden and will be available in the trade as soon as sufficient stock can be propagated. The original plant is about 8 feet tall and nearly 10 feet broad. This variety is somewhat sprawling in habit, the leaves are medium sized and somewhat sparse in number. The inflorescences are large and the flower color unique, being an apple blossom pink in the bud stage and later opening to pure white flowers.

Propagation

Ceanothi can be propagated either by seeds or by cuttings. However, as mentioned earlier, because of the variation within a single species in flower color, leaf shapes and size, and plant habit, as well as the ease by which many of the species hybridize, propagation by seed is unsatisfactory when it is desired to maintain an especially fine plant. To be sure this does not apply to all species, some of which apparently do not hybridize readily and are in general rather uniform in nature. In such cases propagation by seed is to be recommended. Seed collected in the wild will usually be more apt to come true than garden-collected seed. This is certainly the case if the seed is collected from plants which are well isolated from members of other species.

The horticultural varieties mentioned earlier can be propagated only by cuttings and seed should not be collected from these varieties since the resulting plants will usually be inferior to the parent plant.

Most Ceanothus species have a very hard impervious seed coat and, in addition, some apparently have dormant embryos. Consequently, germination may be very slow and uneven if steps are not taken to make the seed coat permeable to air and water. Probably the most satisfactory single treatment, and one that has been used at the Rancho Santa Ana Botanic Garden with good results is to treat the seed with hot water before planting. As mentioned in an earlier chaper, the water is first heated to 180-200°F. and the seed placed in it and allowed to remain in the cooling water for 24 hours before planting. Seeds of *C. sorediatus* and *C. integerrimus* can even be boiled for 1-5 minutes without injury. Some authors recommend stratification of the seeds after the hot water treatment and *C. impressus* is listed as germinating well after 60 days stratification following the hot water treatment. Lammerts reports that he had excellent germination of seeds of 'La Primavera' by treating them with hot water and then allowing them to soak in the water for 5 days before planting.

Great care must be taken in watering the seedlings and young plants since Ceanothi are very susceptible to damping-off. The young plants are probably best held over the first summer in gallon cans and then set out the following winter or early spring.

Propagation by cuttings is discussed in an earlier chapter. In general, tip cuttings should be used and the wood should be partially matured. While the spring months are probably the best time to make cuttings, the exact time when they will root most readily may vary from year to year depending upon environmental conditions.

While more exact details are given later as to the garden requirements of the various species it may be said that in the garden Ceanothi should almost without exception be given a well-drained site, as they cannot tolerate 'wet feet.' This applies to the newer horticultural varieties which, while they will tolerate more summer watering than many of the species, still will not grow in wet, poorly-drained locations.

88

Ceanothus arboreus

CATALINA CEANOTHUS   25 feet   *Ceanothus arboreus*

DESCRIPTION: A large shrub or even a small tree to 25 ft. tall; leaves ovate, pointed, 2-3 in. long, dark green above, whitish on the underside; flower clusters large and well branched, 3-6 in. long, flower buds pinkish opening to pale blue to medium blue flowers.

FLOWERING: February and March.

DISTRIBUTION: Known only from Santa Rosa, Santa Catalina and Santa Cruz Islands.

USES: The Catalina Ceanothus is the largest and one of the most beautiful of the native species. However, due to its size it is best used in large gardens or in native plantings where it is most useful as a tall background shrub or small tree. In recent years this species has been used in roadside plantings. The flowers vary a great deal in color from plant to plant and desirable forms can of course be propagated only by cuttings.

Ceanothus arboreus does best in the coastal areas although it has been grown in a few of the interior valleys. It can tolerate more water than most of the Ceanothi especially if the plants are growing in coarse well-drained soil.

The Catalina Ceanothus was introduced into cultivation by the Southern California Acclimatizing Association of Santa Barbara in 1911 according to Butterfield.

SAN DIEGO LILAC   10 feet   *Ceanothus cyaneus*

DESCRIPTION: An erect evergreen shrub 10 ft. or more tall, often equally broad; leaves alternate, ovate, 1-2 in. long, bright shining green; flower clusters large, 4-10 in. long, somewhat more slender than those of *C. arboreus,* flowers small, very deep rich violet-blue.

FLOWERING: May and June but in cultivation a few flowers may be found nearly all year.

DISTRIBUTION: *Ceanothus cyaneus* is known only from a small area in the interior of San Diego County.

USES: The San Diego Lilac is considered by many as the finest of the Ceanothi and a well-grown shrub when in bloom is a very beautiful sight. Because of its rather large size and because it cannot tolerate summer water, this species should not be attempted in the average small garden. It is quite suitable, however, for native gardens or for planting on dry hillsides, etc. While this plant has been grown to some extent in hot interior areas, it is probably best when grown nearer the coast. *C. cyaneus* blooms later than any of the other species.

Ceanothus cyaneus was first discovered in 1920 and was introduced into cultivation a short time later.

SANTA BARBARA CEANOTHUS 5 feet *Ceanothus impressus*

DESCRIPTION: A rather small densely branched evergreen shrub, 3-5 ft. tall and equally broad; leaves alternate, small, ¼-½ in. long, deep green and very wrinkled; flowers borne in small heads about 1 in. long, flowers deep blue; seed pods rich russet-red.

FLOWERING: March and April.

DISTRIBUTION: *Ceanothus impressus* is known from only a small area in northwestern Santa Barbara County.

USES: *Ceanothus impressus* has been listed as one of the ten best native shrubs in the United States and it is highly recommended for garden use where a medium-sized blue-flowered shrub is desired. This species is one that remains attractive all year whereas a number of the others are rather unattractive during late summer and early fall. Unfortunately *C. impressus* is quite sensitive to summer watering being in this respect similar to *C. cyaneus.* It is a rapidly growing shrub and tends to be somewhat short-lived, so it has been recommended that the plants be replaced about every five years.

This species was first offered for sale by the Calles Nursery of Lompoc in 1934 under another name.

C. impressus var. *nipomensis* is similar to the species except that it is larger growing and reaches a height of as much as 8 feet. The leaves are ½-1 in. long and it blooms about a month earlier than *C. impressus.* This variety is found only in a very small area on Nipomo Mesa in San Luis Obispo County and was first called to the attention of gardeners by Frank J. McCoy.

WESTERN REDBUD   18 feet   *Cercis occidentalis*

DESCRIPTION: A deciduous shrub or small tree 10-18 ft. in height, much-branched from the base, bark smooth, grayish; leaves alternate, nearly round, 2-3½ in. broad, heart-shaped at the base, young leaves glossy-green later becoming darker blue-green; flowers pea-shaped, magenta colored, borne on short stalks in clusters of from 6-12 flowers on wood of the previous season, or on old wood, flowers appearing before the leaves; fruit pods oblong, 1½-3 in. long, ½-¾ in. broad, containing 3-4 seeds, pods often a dull red when mature.

FLOWERING: February to April.

DISTRIBUTION: *Cercis occidentalis* is widespread in California, occurring in the North Coast Ranges from Solano and Napa counties north to Humboldt and Trinity counties, east to Shasta County and south in the Sierra Nevada to Tulare and Kern counties. It is also found in the Laguna and Cuyamaca Mts. in San Diego County.

PROPAGATION: The Western Redbud is propagated from seed which, unless given special treatment, may require several years to germinate. At the Rancho Santa Ana Botanic Garden successful germination has been obtained by pouring hot water (180-200°F.) over the seed and allowing it to soak for 24 hours. Seeds treated in this manner and planted in late fall or early spring have given good germination in about two months. The seed may either be sown in flats or in open beds. If grown in outdoor beds, the plants should remain there for a year and then be transplanted to their permanent location in about February while they are still dormant. In colder areas they may be transplanted when the frost is out of the ground. If grown in flats the seedlings should be transplanted to gallon cans and then planted out the following winter. Growth of the young seedlings is rapid and they often reach a foot or more in height the first season and begin to bloom when they are 3-4 years old.

Cercis occidentalis

91

Cercis occidentalis fruiting

Cercis occidentalis flowering

92

The plants do best in a slightly acid soil which is well drained but they are not especially particular and may be grown in nearly all parts of the state except the deserts. Flowering is most profuse in areas where the temperature goes below 28°F. during the winter. Redbud will take summer irrigation and in inland areas prefers a somewhat shaded location.

Uses: This handsome native can be used in the garden as a specimen plant or as a background for other plants. Due to the magenta color of the flowers, careful consideration should be given to the placing of the plants so that color clashes are avoided.

Western Redbud has been listed as one of the ten best shrubs native to California and according to Rehder it has been in cultivation at least since 1886. It has been available in nurseries in California for a number of years.

MOUNTAIN MAHOGANY   25 feet   *Cercocarpus traskiae*

DESCRIPTION: A large evergreen shrub or small tree to 25 ft. tall, young shoots reddish-brown and thickly covered with hairy down which persists for several years; leaves alternate, broadly elliptic, thick and leathery, coarsely toothed except near the base, 1½-2¼ in. long, dark green above and densely woolly beneath; flowers small, inconspicuous, solitary or few to several in a cluster in the axils of the clustered leaves at the ends of short spur branches; fruit with a long, hairy, twisted tail which gives the fruiting plants a most unusual appearance.

FLOWERING: March to May.

DISTRIBUTION: *Cercocarpus traskiae* is a rare species known only from Santa Catalina and Santa Cruz Islands.

PROPAGATION: Mountain Mahogany is propagated by seeds which may be sown in outside seedbeds during the fall, or they may be planted in flats and the young seedlings transplanted when large enough to handle. The plants will thrive in almost any soil except one that is highly alkaline, and they will tolerate summer irrigation although it is not necessary, as they will grow without it.

Uses: Mountain Mahogany is recommended for native gardens or for dry sunny banks and slopes. It can also be used as a tall informal hedge or as a background for other plantings. The shrubs will stand some pruning and the size can be kept down if the larger branches are removed each year and the basal shoots allowed to develop. During late summer and early fall when the plants are covered with the long-tailed fruits they present a most attractive and at the same time rather unusual appearance.

Cercocarpus traskiae was probably introduced into cultivation in Europe during the first decade of this century. According to Bean it was first grown at the Edinburgh Botanic Garden from seed sent from Santa Catalina Island.

DESERT WILLOW   20 feet   *Chilopsis linearis*

DESCRIPTION: An erect or sprawling shrub or small tree 10-20 ft. high with long willow-like branches; leaves deciduous, narrow, tapering to a point, 2-5 in. long, ¼ in. or less in width, usually alternate; flowers borne in short terminal clusters, individual flower large and showy, 1-2 in. long, Catalpa-like, pink or whitish with purple markings, fragrant; fruit a long narrow pod 4-10 in. long, seeds with a tuft of hairs on either end.

FLOWERING: April to July, or nearer the coast July to September.

DISTRIBUTION: *Chilopsis linearis* is found along dry washes and stream beds in the desert regions of San Diego, Imperial, Riverside, and San Bernardino counties north to Nevada, east to New Mexico and western Texas and south into Mexico.

PROPAGATION: The Desert-Willow may be grown either from seeds or cuttings. The seed, which germinates readily, should be planted thinly, otherwise the seedlings are apt to damp-off. Hardwood cuttings root easily in a mixture of peat moss and sand and at the Rancho Santa Ana Botanic Garden they are placed singly in 4-inch pots to prevent disturbing the young roots.

This shrub is easily grown and will thrive either in a well-drained soil or in clay. It should be given some summer watering since even though the plants are found in desert areas, they occur always where the roots are able to reach water.

USES: The Desert-Willow is highly recommended for use in the dry semi-desert areas of the southwest. It should not be attempted near the coast since the plants apparently need considerable heat to make them bloom well.

There is some variation in flower color in this species and plants for the garden should be grown only from specimens having deeply colored flowers.

According the Rehder it has been in cultivation since before 1800.

Comarostaphylis diversifolia flowers

SUMMER-HOLLY   15 feet   *Comarostaphylis diversifolia*

DESCRIPTION: A large evergreen shrub or small tree as much as 15 feet high; leaves alternate, leathery, elliptical to ovate, 1-3 in. long, dark green, shining above, pubescent below, edge of leaf set with numerous small teeth, leaf margins rolled under except for one form which has leaves that are nearly flat; flowers borne in loose rather short clusters at the

94

tips of the branches, flowers urn-shaped, about ¼ in. long, white and from a distance appearing much like lilies-of-the-valley; fruit a warty round red berry about ¼ in. in diameter.

FLOWERING: March and April; fruit August and September.

DISTRIBUTION: *Comarostaphylis diversifolia* is found on Santa Rosa, Santa Cruz and Santa Catalina Islands and along the coast from Santa Barbara County south to San Diego County.

PROPAGATION: Summer-Holly is propagated by seeds which may be sown in flats during the fall in a mixture of sandy loam and leafmold. Germination usually occurs within a couple of months and the young seedlings should be ready to place into individual containers during early spring. After that growth is rapid and the plants should be transferred to gallon cans before they become rootbound. By fall the plants will be 8-12 inches tall and ready to set into their permanent locations. In southern California Summer-Holly probably grows best in light shade in a coarse, well-drained soil. However, at this garden the plants have done fairly well in heavy adobe and full sun. Irrigation during the summer months may be occasional, however this species is quite drought resistant and once established can get along with only the moisture received as rainfall.

USES: Summer-Holly is well suited for garden use where it may be of value for background, screen, or hedge plantings. It will stand some pruning and the plants can be made to remain compact shrubs or allowed to become taller and more tree-like in form. Summer-Holly is not as well known as some California native shrubs but experience at the Rancho Santa Ana Botanic Garden, as well as in the San Francisco Bay area, has shown its value as a garden plant which is not only most attractive when in bloom but is also very striking again during August and September when it is covered with its bright red berries.

Little is known about the horticultural history of this plant. Rehder gives 1926 as the date when it was introduced into cultivation but it seems quite possible that it was grown before that time.

Comarostaphylis diversifolia fruit

ISLAND TREE-POPPY   20 feet   *Dendromecon harfordii*

DESCRIPTION: A freely branched evergreen shrub 2 feet to as much as 20 feet tall with shreddy bark on the stems and larger branches; leaves alternate, broadly elliptical to oval, 1-3 in. long, leathery, gray or yellowish-green, leaf margins smooth; flowers large, attractive, terminating the branchlets, petals usually 4, bright yellow, ¾-1¼ in. long, stamens numerous; fruit a long narrow curved capsule 2-4 in. long.

FLOWERING: April to June but a few flowers may be produced anytime during the year.

DISTRIBUTION: *Dendromecon harfordii* is known only from the Santa Barbara Islands.

PROPAGATION: The Island Tree-Poppy may be grown either from seeds or cuttings. The seed, which is often difficult to germinate, is best handled by planting it in flats in a light soil mixture after which straw or pine needles are placed over the surface of the soil and then burned. The flats should then be watered thoroughly. Young seedlings will usually appear in about a month and they may be transplanted to small pots when large enough to handle and still later moved to gallon cans. They will usually be ready for planting in their permanent locations the following winter. It has been reported that this shrub can be propagated from well-ripened firm summer shoots placed in very sandy soil and given moderate heat. Cuttings, however, have not been attempted at this Botanic Garden.

In the garden the plants should be given a coarse soil and provided with excellent drainage. They thrive best if given full sun and little or no water during the summer months. The Tree-Poppy can also be grown in heavy soils but it will usually be rather short-lived.

USES: The Island Tree-Poppy is certainly one of the most distinctive and showy of our native shrubs and it is highly recommended for larger native gardens. In the ordinary garden this plant can be recommended only if its cultural requirements can be met, the most important of which is absolute dryness during the summer months. Dendromecon

Dendromecon harfordii

96

will withstand considerable pruning and it can be maintained at any size desired. It is most attractive when used as a specimen plant but it can be very valuable in other ways.

It is not known when the Island Tree-Poppy was first grown in a garden. The mainland species, *Dendromecon rigida,* which is in many ways similar to the Island species, was first discovered by Douglas and was introduced into cultivation from seed collected by Wm. Lobb in 1854.

DIPLACUS

In the California flora there are few plants which produce a greater display of flowers over a longer period of time or in a greater array of colors than do the Bush Monkey Flowers. These soft-wooded evergreen shrubs and subshrubs vary from about 1-3 ft. in height and are usually about as broad as tall. McMinn in his recent account of the group[1] now recognizes some 14 different entities, almost all of them of interest to the gardener. However, in southern California D. *longifolius,* D. *longifolius* var. *rutilis* (D. *rutilis* of McMinn), D. *grandiflorus,* D. *puniceus,* and D. *aridus* are probably the most important. Since the various species hybridize readily both in the garden and in the wild, many of the plants being sold today are actually hybrids. This is not to be deplored since through hybridization numerous new and unusual colors have been developed which make them all the more interesting for the gardener.

Propagation

Except perhaps for D. *clevelandii,* little difficulty will be experienced in growing the various Bush Monkey Flowers and the plants are quite tolerant of different soil conditions. The seeds, which are very small, should be sown thinly in pots or flats and the seedlings transplanted to individual containers when they are large enough to handle. Care should be exercised in watering the seedlings since they are rather susceptible to damping-off. By the time they are 3-4 in. high they can be planted in the garden. They should be irrigated carefully until they become established, after which time watering should be reduced. However, small amounts of water will prolong the blooming season which lasts for several months.

Seed sown during the late fall will produce plants which will bloom profusely the following summer. Unfortunately after flowering the plants become rather unattractive, however, if they are pruned to within 3-4 in. of the ground and then watered they will send up new growth and will bloom a second time. Another pruning the following winter will insure an abundance of flowers the next spring. It is doubtful if the plants should be held longer than that. Young plants placed in the garden early in the spring will bloom after the older ones have finished and have been removed. If the gardener will allow a few capsules to mature on an unusually fine individual he will have sufficient seed to replant whenever necessary.

Diplacus can also be propagated by cuttings, but it is doubtful if this method is to be recommended except for reproducing named horticultural hybrids which cannot be propagated otherwise, such as McMinn's 'Blanche McInnes' and 'Grandrutilis'.

The plants grow well in most types of soil except those which are too rich. They can be given full sun or light shade and many of the hybrids are better if grown in light shade since intense sunlight causes many of the flowers to fade. This is especially true of the orange- and bronze-colored hybrids.

---

[1]H. E. McMinn. *Studies in the Genus Diplacus (Scrophulariaceae).* Madroño 11: 33-128, 1951.

JACUMBA DIPLACUS 18 inches *Diplacus aridus*

DESCRIPTION: A low subshrub 8-18 in. tall often spreading as much as 2 ft., stems usually straw-colored, leaves ¾-1¾ in. long and ¼-⅞ in. wide, usually more or less elliptic, margins slightly toothed, leaves without hairs but glutinous; flowers 1½-2 in. long, pale yellow, 2-lipped although less obviously so than in the other species, lobes usually recurved.

DISTRIBUTION: *Diplacus aridus* is known from only a few locations in southeastern San Diego County and adjacent Baja California.

AZALEA-FLOWERED DIPLACUS 2½ feet *Diplacus grandiflorus*

DESCRIPTION: A spreading subshrub ¾-2½ ft. tall spreading 1-3 ft., leaves 1-2½ in. long and ¼-¾ in. wide, oblong-elliptic to elliptic, the leaves smooth and free from hairs but somewhat glutinous; flowers numerous, large, 2¼-2¾ in. long, 2-lipped, buff-colored. The lobes of the corolla usually deeply notched differing in this respect from the other species except *D. fasciculatus* which some authors include under *D. grandiflorus*.

DISTRIBUTION: *Diplacus grandiflorus* is found on the western slope of the Sierra Nevada in Plumas, Butte, Yuba, Sierra, Nevada, and Placer counties.

Diplacus aridus

Diplacus puniceus

Diplacus longiflorus var. rutilis

SOUTHERN DIPLACUS   4 feet   *Diplacus longiflorus*

DESCRIPTION: An erect, much-branched shrub 1-4 ft. tall; leaves 1-3½ in. long, ¼-¾ in. wide, lanceolate to linear-lanceolate or oblong, upper surface nearly smooth, lower surface covered with hairs, margins set with small teeth or nearly smooth toward the base; flowers two-lipped, 2-2½ in. long, variable in color from almost white to orange-yellow.

DISTRIBUTION: *Diplacus longiflorus* occurs along coastal southern California from San Luis Obispo County south to Orange County. It is found also on Santa Cruz and Santa Rosa Islands as well as in a few scattered localities in Baja California, San Diego, Riverside, Kern, Monterey and San Benito counties.

D. longiflorus var. *rutilis* is similar to *D. longiflorus* except that the flowers in the pure form are a deep velvety red. It is found in southwestern Ventura, Los Angeles, and western Riverside counties. Due to hybridization between the variety *rutilis* and the species itself, numerous intermediate colors are often found in nature.

SCARLET-FLOWERED DIPLACUS   5 feet   *Diplacus puniceus*

DESCRIPTION: An erect shrub 1½-5 ft. tall often with reddish branches, leaves 1-3 in. long and ⅛-½ in. wide, leaves lanceolate to elliptic, upper surface glabrous, lower surface glabrous or covered with fine hairs, margins entire or finely toothed; flowers 1¼-1¾ in. long, 2-lipped, brick-red to orange-red.

DISTRIBUTION: *Diplacus puniceus* is found in western San Diego County and adjacent Baja California and in Orange and Riverside counties. It occurs also on Santa Catalina Island.

ST. CATHERINE'S LACE   8 feet   *Eriogonum giganteum*

DESCRIPTION: An evergreen shrub 5-8 ft. high, usually broader than tall, old trunk covered with rough shreddy bark, young branches gray pubescent; leaves alternate, often clustered at the tips of the branches, leaves ovate, 2-4 in. long and up to 2 in. wide, margins wavy, young leaves densely white-hairy but later the upper surface becomes somewhat smooth and greenish while the conspicuously veined undersurface remains gray; inflorescence large, 1-3 ft. long and equally broad, borne well above the leaves, much-branched, the individual flower clusters soft grayish, flat, the entire inflorescence producing a lacy canopy over the plant, individual flowers minute, petals lacking, calyx of 6 segments in two series of 3 each, the inner segments each with a pink nerve.

FLOWERING: June and July.

DISTRIBUTION: *Eriogonum giganteum* is known only from Santa Catalina and San Clemente Islands where it occurs on steep rocky dry slopes.

PROPAGATION: St. Catherine's Lace is propagated by seeds which may be sown in flats during late fall or early spring. The young seedlings should be transplanted when very small since the plants early develop a long taproot which makes it difficult to move them at a later time without considerable loss. The young plants should then be set out into the garden before they become root-bound. At the Rancho Santa Ana Botanic Garden many have been established by merely broadcasting the seed during late fall or early winter. This method has been very satisfactory since they appear to do better than when grown in pots or cans. They can be expected to bloom the second season and in favorable areas they will readily volunteer.

In the garden this shrub prefers a coarse well-drained soil with full sun and little or no water after it becomes established. If grown in heavy soil it should not be watered during the summer. The appearance of the plants will be improved if the inflorescences are removed after the flowering period.

USES: St. Catherine's Lace is a most unusual and attractive plant and is highly recommended for larger gardens where its cultural requirements can be met. There is no other large California native which produces such a lacy, airy effect as this species does during its blooming season and as a specimen shrub it can be quite spectacular. Its charm comes from its form and texture rather than from its color which is an overall soft gray-green.

Due to its habit of growth the plants require careful pruning in order to keep them attractive during the seasons of the year when they are not in bloom.

The inflorescences can be used for home decoration and they will remain a pleasing arrangement indefinitely without water but will shatter badly if disturbed. In bright light they will take on soft hues of tan, rust, and brown.

St. Catherine's Lace was introduced into cultivation at least before 1900 since a photograph of a large specimen growing in the garden of the Southern California Acclimatizing Association at Santa Barbara was published in the Gardeners' Chronicle for that year.

PHOTOGRAPH BY PERCY EVERETT

Eriogonum giganteum

101

Fallugia paradoxa fruit

Fallugia paradoxa flowers

APACHE PLUME   5 feet   *Fallugia paradoxa*

DESCRIPTION: A much-branched deciduous shrub 1-5 ft. tall with flaky bark; leaves alternate and borne in clusters along the branchlets, leaves ½-1 in. long, divided into from 3-5, or even 7, long narrow divisions, the edges of the ultimate divisions rolled under, leaves rusty on the underside; flowers large, white, 1-1½ in. in diameter and usually borne singly at the ends of the branches, petals 5, stamens numerous; fruit composed of numerous achenes each with a long plumose tail 1-1½ in. long.

FLOWERING: April and May.

DISTRIBUTION: *Fallugia paradoxa* is found on dry slopes in the mountains of eastern San Bernardino County, east to western Texas, north to southern Utah and Colorado, and south into Mexico.

PROPAGATION: Apache Plume is grown from seed which may be sown in flats and the seedlings later transplanted. It has been reported that the seed germinates well only with a temperature of from 60-70°F. While no experiments have been conducted, experience at this garden has been that the best germination took place when the seed was sown in September, a period when the temperature might well be within the 60-70°F. range.

In the garden the plants should be given a well-drained soil and either full sun or partial shade. At the Botanic Garden they have usually looked better when grown in light shade. They will stand severe pruning which should be done during the winter.

USES: Apache Plume is recommended mainly for native gardens where it is quite a satisfactory deciduous shrub and one that is pleasing in appearance both when in flower and again when fruiting.

Fallugia paradoxa was introduced into cultivation in 1877.

SOUTHERN FREMONTIA   20 feet   *Fremontia mexicana*

DESCRIPTION: An evergreen shrub 10-20 ft. high, often tree-like in age with a single trunk 2-4 in. in diameter or the plants may be much-branched from the base, young branches, foliage and flower parts strongly pubescent with stellate hairs (a stalked hair at the tip of which there are ray-like projections), branches flexible; leaves alternate, lobed, ovate, oblong or elliptic, 1-3 in. long, variously 3-5-lobed, dark green above and rusty-pubescent below; flowers borne along the branches in the axils of the leaves, individual flowers large, 2½-3½ in. in diameter, bowl-shaped, petals absent but the fused calyx corolla-like, color a rich deep orange-yellow to reddish-orange on the outside and a clear yellow inside, stamens 5; fruit an ovoid, acutely pointed capsule which is covered with a thick matting of stellate hairs, seeds shiny, black, about ⅛ in. long.

FLOWERING: Peak bloom is reached in April but flowers may appear as early as February and as late as June. In cultivation a few blossoms may be produced occasionally throughout the year.

DISTRIBUTION: *Fremontia mexicana* is found on dry slopes in extreme southern San Diego County (Otay Mt.) and south into Baja California.

PROPAGATION: Fremontia is propagated by seed which is often difficult to germinate. In order to hasten the process, the seeds should first have their hard seed-coat softened or partially removed by sandpapering or by soaking them in a weak lye solution. At the Botanic Garden successful germination has been speeded by treating the seeds with hot water (180-200°F.) before planting them. It is also advisable to plant the seed directly into small containers such as 4-inch pots in order to avoid losses in transplanting the young

Fremontia mexicana

seedlings. The potting soil should be a coarse well-drained mixture with little humus and the young plants should not be allowed to become root-bound.

Fremontias are difficult to propagate by cuttings. Except for the difficulty involved it would, however, be a most desirable method since Fremontias vary to a certain extent in nature and the use of cuttings would make possible increase of the better forms.

In the garden it is essential that these shrubs be given a coarse, very well-drained soil if the plantings are to succeed. The young plants should be put out during the late fall or winter in order that they may become established before summer, thus avoiding the necessity of excessive irrigation of the plants during the summer months. After establishment they should receive no water at all during the summer.

In heavy soil or under conditions of excessive watering they will grow rapidly for a time but after a year or so they will suddenly die. Hansen and Thomas of the University of California in studying the diseases of Fremontia[1] concluded that a stem girdling caused by the common plant pathogene *Phytopthora cactorum* is responsible for many of the losses in gardens. They describe the disease as killing the bark around the stem commonly at or near the ground-line, but occasionally higher up, and the death of the bark is followed by withering of the entire plant. They concluded that this disease seems to be clearly related to excess water and they recommend that plantings be made in exceptionally well-drained areas and that water be applied very sparingly. Another disease is described by these authors in which the fungus invades the water-carrying vessels of the plant causing it to be stunted and the leaves to wilt and soon drop. They also describe two leaf-spot diseases but neither of these is important since they do not cause the death of the host.

USES: *Fremontia mexicana* is always named in any list of the 10 best shrubs of California and it has also been included as one of the 10 best shrubs native to the United States. When it is in bloom it certainly is as beautiful as any exotic shrub. However, it is a plant that can be recommended to gardeners only if its cultural requirements can be met. It is unfortunate that this, one of the finest of all California natives, is also one of the most difficult to maintain permanently.

It is largely through the efforts of Kate Sessions and Theodore Payne that this species was extensively propagated and has become one of the most popular of California shrubs. It was first listed in a catalogue by Payne in 1919.

Another species of *Fremontia* which is often grown is *F. californica*. It differs from *F. mexicana* mainly in having smaller flowers, 1¼-2½ in. in diameter which are more nearly flat when open than those of *mexicana* and the flowers are a clear yellow lacking the trace of red on the outside. This species also has smaller and thinner leaves than *mexicana*. The flowers are displayed to better advantage than they are in *mexicana* and from a distance the plant reminds one of Forsythia, a fact that was noted by Hooker when he described the species in the Botanical Magazine in 1866. *F. californica* appears to stand a small amount of summer water whereas *F. mexicana* does not. *F. californica* is found on dry slopes from central California south to the western edge of the Colorado Desert and the southern slopes of the San Bernardino and San Gabriel Mts.

Fremontia californica has long been in cultivation, having bloomed for the first time in England in 1854 from seed sent from California by a Mr. Wrench.

Cultural recommendations are the same as for *F. mexicana*.

During recent years some of the plants offered by nurseries have appeared to be intermediate between *F. mexicana* and *F. californica* and it was suspected that they might be of hybrid origin. Controlled hybrids were produced at the Botanic Garden and when they bloomed it became apparent that they were very similar to some of the plants being sold as *F. mexicana*. It would seem that natural hybridization can be expected when the two species are grown near one another. Since some nurserymen have obtained seed from the Botanic Garden where both species are being grown it is not unnatural that some of the

---

[1] H. N. Hansen, and H. Earl Thomas. 1945. *Diseases of Fremontia*, Madroño 8: 39-42.

resulting plants should prove to be hybrids. It has been our experience that some of the hybrids are more beautiful than either species. It is unfortunate that these plants are so difficult to grow from cuttings otherwise the fine hybrid forms would be recommended rather than the species.

Fremontia californica × *F. mexicana*

OCOTILLO   25 feet   *Fouquieria splendens*

DESCRIPTION: A thorny shrub with several to many long whip-like stems from the base, stems mostly unbranched, 8-25 ft. tall, gray with darker furrows; primary leaves fleshy, egg-shaped, ⅜-1 in. long, soon deciduous, the petiole (the stalk portion of a leaf) developing into a thorn in the axil of which later appear fascicles of secondary leaves; flowers borne in a cluster 4-12 in. long at the tip of the stem, flowers tubular, ¾-1 in. long, scarlet, lobes of the corolla recurved.

FLOWERING: In the summer after the rains.

DISTRIBUTION: *Fouquieria splendens* is found on dry slopes and mesas below 2500 ft. elevation in the Colorado Desert, the eastern part of the Mojave Desert, east to Texas and south into Mexico.

PROPAGATION: Ocotillo is propagated by cuttings taken during the winter or early spring and either placed in individual containers or put directly into the ground where they are to grow. The soil should be coarse and well-drained and the plants should have full sun.

USES: Ocotillo is well known to all who are acquainted with the desert and it is a plant which has probably been more often used for practical reasons than as an ornamental. In

106

the desert it is often grown to form a living fence—a most suitable material since it soon becomes impenetrable. It has also been used in the construction of small inclosures, etc. It has, however, considerable value as an ornamental in desert areas and when it is in bloom it is very attractive. Ocotillo can, however, be grown in other areas than the desert and it has done well at the Rancho Santa Ana Botanic Garden both in Orange County and at Claremont.

Regarding its introduction into cultivation, nothing is known. Undoubtedly it has been used for a long period of time by those living in the areas of the Southwest where it grows. It is known that the fruit capsules, as well as the flowers, were used as a source of food by certain Indian tribes.

Fouquieria splendens

107

ISLAND BUSH-SNAPDRAGON   4 feet   *Galvezia speciosa*

DESCRIPTION: A brittle-stemmed evergreen shrub to as much as 3-5 ft. across, usually broader than tall although when clambering over other shrubs the plants may reach 7-8 ft.; leaves opposite or 3 at each node, oval or oblong in shape, 1-1¼ in. long, ⅜-½ in. wide, thick and leathery, margins smooth; flowers borne singly in the axils of the upper leaves forming clusters of from 5-20 flowers at the tips of the branches, flowers snapdragon-like, scarlet, 1 in. long.

FLOWERING: April and May, but some flowers are produced nearly all year.

DISTRIBUTION: *Galvezia speciosa* is known only from Santa Catalina, San Clemente and Guadalupe Islands where it is found in rocky canyons.

PROPAGATION: Either seeds or cuttings is a satisfactory and easy method of propagation. Seed may be sown in flats and later transplanted to pots or cans before being set into their permanent locations. Cuttings 4-6 in. long root readily at nearly all seasons of the year. After rooting the cuttings should be potted in a loamy soil mixture and held for a time before planting out which is best done in late fall or early spring. *Galvezia speciosa* prefers a coarse, loamy, well-drained soil but it will grow in heavy clay fairly well. After establishment the plants should be given very little or no water during the summer months.

In the coastal areas Bush-Snapdragon will grow in sun or shade, however, it will bloom more profusely if given considerable sun. In inland areas the plants should always have partial shade.

Galvezia speciosa

Uses: Bush-Snapdragon can be used in mixed plantings, as a low filler plant, and it is especially useful for planting on partially shaded banks. As is true for many natives, it should be judiciously pruned from time to time in order to keep the plants attractive. It is probably by nature a rather short-lived plant and it should be replaced after a few years.

Galvezia speciosa

Two forms of this species are known, one having hairy leaves and the other smooth, shining leaves. The latter form is to be preferred for garden planting, not only because of the more pleasing appearance, but also the hairy-leaved form appears to be susceptible to a leaf-spot disease which detracts from the handsomeness of the plants.

Nothing is known regarding the horticultural history of this plant. It has been grown at the Rancho Santa Ana Botanic Garden since 1927.

Garrya elliptica

SILK TASSEL BUSH 10 feet *Garrya elliptica*

DESCRIPTION: An evergreen shrub 5-10 ft. high, or occasionally a small tree up to 20 ft. tall; leaves opposite, elliptical or oval, 1½-3 in. long and 1-1½ in. wide, thick and leathery, upper surface dark shining green, lower surface covered with dense woolly hair, leaf margins wavy and with a tendency to curl under; flowers borne in long dangling silvery-gray catkins which appear during the winter, the male or staminate catkins 3-7 in. long or sometimes longer, female or pistillate catkins shorter; fruit a round berry ½-⅜ in. in diameter, densely hairy, becoming nearly smooth in age.

FLOWERING: December to February.

DISTRIBUTION: *Garrya elliptica* is found in the Coast Ranges from Oregon southward to San Luis Obispo County, rarely farther south.

PROPAGATION: The Silk-Tassel Bush may be grown either from seeds or cuttings or by layering. However, at the Rancho Santa Ana Botanic Garden it has been propagated solely from seed which is slow to germinate. Planted in flats in a sandy loam during late fall or winter, germination will take place in from two to three months. Mirov and Kraebel recommend 3-months stratification, while McMinn recommends treating the seed with a lye solution for 24 hours after which the seeds are washed and sown and kept in a cool lath house for about three months after which the flats are removed to a higher temperature. Seedlings grow rapidly and should be transplanted to individual containers when they are large enough to handle. This species thrives best in well-drained soil and it may be planted in sun or partial shade. In southern California it should be placed in a protected spot with partial shade, otherwise the sun and hot winds tend to scorch the leaves and the plants become unsightly. If, however, they are damaged they may be cut back and will then send up vigorous new growth.

USES: The Silk-Tassel Bush with its dark green, almost oak-like, evergreen leaves is a desirable shrub the entire year but when it is covered with its long silvery-gray catkins during the winter months when little else is in bloom, it is an unusual sight which always brings comments from all who see it. Unfortunately in southern California it does not thrive as well or bloom as profusely as it does farther north, probably because the winter temperatures are not low enough for it. At the Botanic Garden a few plants bloomed profusely after the cold winter of 1948-49. This species should not be planted in areas far removed from the coast.

Garrya elliptica was introduced into cultivation in 1828 from seed collected by Douglas and it was sold in California by Wm. Walker of San Francisco as early as 1860.

TOYON 15 feet *Heteromeles arbutifolia*

DESCRIPTION: A large erect bushy evergreen shrub 6-15 ft. or more tall; leaves alternate, oblong or elliptical, 2-4 in. long, ¾-1½ in. wide, thick and leathery, dark glossy green above, lighter below, leaf margins set with small saw-like teeth; flowers produced in large flat-topped clusters, individual flowers small, white, followed by clusters of holly-like berries ¼ in. or more in diameter which remain on the bushes for some time.

FLOWERING: June and July; fruit November to February.

DISTRIBUTION: *Heteromeles arbutifolia* is found from near sea-level to 3500 ft. elevation in the lower Sierra Nevada from Shasta and Tehama counties to Tulare County, and in the Coast Ranges from Humboldt County south to Baja California. It is also found on Santa Catalina and San Clemente Islands.

Heteromeles arbutifolia

PROPAGATION: Toyon can be propagated either from seed or from tip cuttings taken in the fall or spring. Since there is considerable variation between plants of this species, especially fine forms should be propagated by the cuttings. The correct time to take them is when the wood is partially matured but when it will still snap when broken

Plants are easily grown from seed planted in flats and germination takes place in from two to three weeks. Seedlings should be transplanted when large enough to handle and the plants are best held in the lath house the first season and planted out during the following fall. Toyon is less particular as to soil and water than are many native shrubs and provided with good drainage it can withstand considerable summer moisture. The first

Heteromeles arbutifolia flowers

Heteromeles arbutifolia fruit

season after it is set out it should be irrigated occasionally until it has become established. The plants may be grown in either full sun or partial shade.

Some growers have had trouble with the leaves being attacked by a fungus during the period when the plants were in the lath house or shortly thereafter. According to Van Dersal this disease can be controlled by Bordeaux spray. However, it was not effective when used at this Botanic Garden.

USES: Probably no California shrub is so well known as Toyon (also known as California Holly, or Christmas Berry) and when it is covered with its clusters of bright red berries it is probably the most beautiful of our native shrubs. It is commonly used for decoration during the Christmas season and large quantities of it are sent to the Eastern markets.

Toyon has been extensively planted in California during the past several decades. In gardens it can be used either as a large shrub or pruned to form a small tree but it is probably most attractive when used as a specimen plant.

Two varieties of Toyon have been named; a yellow-fruited form has been called variety *cerina*, and a form from Catalina which has larger fruits than the mainland form has been called variety *macrocarpa*. Both these varieties are available at nurseries in California. Variety *macrocarpa* is considered as the finest horticulturally although for some decorating purposes it is not as desirable as the species because the clusters of berries are so heavy that the branches cannot hold them erect and they tend to droop when used in arrangements.

Heteromeles arbutifolia (*Photinia arbutifolia* according to some authors) was first collected by Haenke in 1791 probably near Monterey and it was introduced into cultivation by Archibald Menzies in 1796.

114

BLADDER-POD   4 feet   *Isomeris arborea*

DESCRIPTION: A much-branched rounded evergreen shrub 3-4 ft. high; leaves gray-green, alternate, divided into 3 leaflets, the leaflets oblong to more or less elliptic, ¼-1½ in. long; flowers yellow, borne in dense terminal clusters, individual flower ⅜-⅝ in. long, 4-petalled; fruit a conspicuously inflated leathery capsule, ¾-2 in. long, variable in shape from elliptic-oblong to nearly round, seeds few in number, large.

FLOWERING: February to May with a few flowers throughout the year.

DISTRIBUTION: *Isomeris arborea* is found on bluffs and hillsides in coastal regions from central California to Baja California and also about the western edge of both the Mojave and Colorado deserts.

PROPAGATION: Seeds sown in flats or in the open ground during the fall often germinate within a week or ten days. If grown in a flat the young seedlings should be transplanted to individual containers when they are large enough to handle. In favorable areas this species readily volunteers.

In the garden the plants are not particular as to soil but they should not be heavily watered during the summer months.

Isomeris arborea

115

USES: This species is not recommended for the average garden but is a most useful low shrub for producing masses of color during the spring months and it can be used advantageously in larger native gardens, or for planting on dry slopes and road banks since it is quite drought resistant and it will grow with no more water than it receives from natural rainfall.

Bladder-Pod was first collected by Nuttall who also collected seeds of the plant which he turned over to a Mr. Buist of Philadelphia who in turn sent some of them to the Royal Botanic Garden at Edinburgh in 1839.

Leptodactylon californicum

PRICKLY PHLOX 3½ feet *Leptodactylon californicum*

DESCRIPTION: A much-branched evergreen shrub 1-3½ feet tall; foliage dense and fascicled, heath-like, leaves alternate, prickly, each divided into from 5-9 narrow sharp-pointed segments; flowers borne in congested terminal clusters often in such numbers as to hide the leaves, flowers pink to rose-red, occasionally white, phlox-like with a narrow tube ¾-1 in. long and with 5 corolla-lobes about ⅝ in. long.

FLOWERING: February to July.

DISTRIBUTION: *Leptodactylon californicum* is found in the chaparral in the Santa Monica Mts. and in Ventura, Santa Barbara and Monterey counties. The variety *glandulosum*, which is horticulturally the same as the species except for having glandular hairs on the upper parts of the plant, is common below 3000 ft. elevation from Banning and the Santa Ana Mts. to Los Angeles.

PROPAGATION: Prickly Phlox may be grown either from seed or cuttings. Seed sown in flats during the autumn germinates in about a week and the seedlings can be moved to individual containers when they are large enough to handle. The plants should flower within a year. English growers report that this species is easily propagated from young tip cuttings inserted thickly in a pot which is then covered with a bell jar.

In the garden the plants should be given a very coarse well-drained soil with no water during the summer.

USES: Prickly Phlox is an extremely fine looking plant when in flower but there are some limitations to its use in the garden. It tends to become sprawly and lose the foliage from its lower parts. Too, this species is apparently short-lived and according to McMinn in nature probably does not live more than 3-6 years. For the reasons given above and also because of its demand for dryness during the summer, it is not recommended for the average garden. For native gardens it can be used most effectively especially on dry rocky slopes. In such favorable areas it will readily volunteer.

Prickly Phlox was introduced into cultivation from seed collected by Wm. Lobb near San Bernardino which he sent to the Veitch nursery in England. There it bloomed for the first time in 1855. However, it soon disappeared from cultivation and it was not re-introduced into England until 1925. There it is often used as a pot plant and one grower reports six-hundred open flowers on a plant grown in a 7-inch pot.

TWINBERRY HONEYSUCKLE 10 feet *Lonicera involucrata*

DESCRIPTION: A deciduous shrub 2-10 ft. tall and usually equally broad, branches slender and wand-like; leaves opposite, 2-5 in. long and 1-2½ in. wide, oblong to egg-shaped tapering to a point, smooth dark green above, under side lighter in color and hairy, leaf margins smooth; flowers borne on slender stalks 1-2 in. long in the axils of the leaves, flowers tubular, yellow, ½-¾ in. long, always in pairs surrounded by 2 showy bracts which may be greenish-to wine-red in color and often appearing petal-like; fruits a shiny black berry, oval or round, about ⅓ in. in diameter.

FLOWERING: March to July.

DISTRIBUTION: *Lonicera involucrata* occurs in moist shady places at altitudes of from sea level to 9500 ft. In the Sierra Nevada it is found from Modoc County south to Tulare County and in the Coast Ranges from Del Norte County south to Santa Barbara County. It is also widely distributed in other parts of North America.

PROPAGATION: The Twinberry Honeysuckle may be grown from seeds and cuttings or by dividing old clumps. Seeds are usually slow to germinate unless they have been stratified for several months. Cuttings of mature wood taken in February root easily in sand after which they may be placed in containers or set into their permanent locations. Old clumps are best divided while the plants are dormant. This species is not particular as to soil type but should be given ample water and in southern California does best if given partial shade. Since the greatest profusion of flowers is on young vigorous shoots, pruning should consist of removing the older branches, cutting them off near the base.

Lonicera involucrata is not restricted to California in its distribution but extends through the Rocky Mts. and as far north as Quebec and Alaska and as far south as Mexico. Over its range there is considerable variation in the species and the coastal form which occurs from Santa Barbara County north to Del Norte County has been described by some as a separate species, *Lonicera ledebourii* and by others as a variety of *involucrata, Lonicera involucrata* var. *ledebourii*. This coastal form is considered as the most desirable one for ornamental planting purposes.

USES: The Twinberry Honeysuckle can be used for mixed plantings, along pool edges, or in other moist spots where there is some shade.

This species was introduced into cultivation in 1824 by William Williams from plants growing in Canada. The coastal form was first grown about 1838.

Lonicera involucrata

BLUE BUSH LUPINE   5 feet   *Lupinus longifolius*

DESCRIPTION: A stout erect much-branched shrub 2½-5 ft. high; leaves with short petioles and with from 6-9 leaflets, the largest up to 2 in. long, sparingly hairy on both surfaces; flowers in narrow spike-like inflorescences 8-16 in. long, individual flowers pea-shaped, ½-¾ in. long, bluish; fruit pods yellowish, 1½-2½ in. long.

FLOWERING: March to June with the greatest number of flowers during April and May.

118

DISTRIBUTION: *Lupinus longifolius* is found on dry hillsides along the coast from Los Angeles County south to San Diego County and inland as far as San Dimas and Campo.

PROPAGATION: By seed which may be slow to germinate and it is suggested that they be treated with hot water, chipped with a knife, or sandpapered in order to bring about better germination. In any case, it is probably best to sow directly into 4-in. pots in a light sandy soil mixture placing several seeds in each pot and later removing all except one seedling. Seedlings should be planted into the ground before they become the least pot-bound or before the taproot has grown through the hole in the bottom of the pot.

In the garden this species should be given a sunny location in a coarse well-drained soil and no summer irrigation after the plants are once established. They normally bloom the first season.

USES: This species is probably the most satisfactory of the bush lupines for use in this area and when well grown is a most striking thing with its many erect, candle-like spikes of blue flowers all over the plant. It is of restricted use, however, due to its cultural requirements and therefore not recommended to the average gardener. The plants are by nature short-lived and plans should be made to replace them every few years.

Lupinus longifolius

Myrica californica

WAX MYRTLE

30 feet

Myrica californica

DESCRIPTION: A much-branched evergreen shrub or small tree 8-30 ft. tall, bark gray, young branches at first hairy; leaves 2-4 in. long and ½-¾ in. wide, narrow, oval or elliptical, tapering at both ends, dark glossy green, leathery, resinous-dotted on the under side, margins of leaf regularly toothed, leaves slightly fragrant when crushed; inflorescence in the form of small catkins, male and female flowers borne in separate catkins but on the same plant; fruit small, roundish, purplish and covered with a white waxy bloom.

FLOWERING: March and April.

DISTRIBUTION: *Myrica californica* occurs on sand dunes and moist hillsides near the coast from the Santa Monica Mts. north to the Puget Sound.

PROPAGATION: Wax Myrtle can be grown either from seeds or cuttings. Cuttings root rather easily especially if they are first treated with one of the root-promoting hormones. The seeds, which are slow to germinate, should be sown in flats and the flats kept well watered until germination takes place. Mirov and Kraebel report good germination if the seeds are first stratified for three months. The young seedlings may be transplanted to 2-inch pots when they are an inch or so tall and later transplanted to gallon cans. It is important that they not be allowed to dry out especially when they are in the small pots.

In the garden the plants thrive best in a rather rich soil which contains considerable humus and they can be grown either in full sun or partial shade. This species requires water during the summer and under garden conditions it is considered as slow-growing.

USES: Wax Myrtle is recommended for gardens in the coastal areas and it should not be planted in the hot interior valleys. This shrub is most satisfactory for use as a background plant, for foundation planting, as a specimen shrub, and it is especially useful as a hedge.

According to Rehder it was introduced into cultivation in 1849.

PARRY'S NOLINA

4 feet (8-10 feet when in flower)

Nolina parryi

DESCRIPTION: A large perennial, stemless or with a woody stem several feet high in old plants topped by a large cluster of many narrow leaves 2-5 ft. long and about 1 in. wide, leaves dull green, stiff or flexuous, edges set with small sharp teeth with a sharp spine at the tip of the leaf; inflorescence a large panicle with thousands of small flowers borne at the top of a stalk often 4-6 ft. high, staminate and pistillate flowers produced on separate plants, staminate flowers borne on slender pedicels, flowers creamy-white, composed of 6 segments opening to form a low bowl-shaped flower ¼ in. in diameter, pistillate flowers similar but smaller, greenish; fruit a capsule about ½ in. broad with 3 flattened straw-colored wings.

FLOWERING: May and June.

DISTRIBUTION: *Nolina parryi* is found on dry slopes on the western edge of the Colorado Desert, Little San Bernardino Mts., Chuckawalla Mts., west to the Santa Ana Mts., east to Arizona and south to Baja California.

PROPAGATION: Propagation of this species is by seed which may be sown either in deep flats or in outdoor seedbeds. The seed germinates within a couple of weeks and the young plants may later be transplanted to individual containers and in less than a year they will be ready for their permanent locations. In the garden Nolina should be given a site with full sun and while it grows best in a rocky well-drained soil it will do fairly well in heavy soil if the plants are not watered during the summer months. They will, however, require

121

water and attention for the first year after they have been set out. At the Rancho Santa Ana Botanic Garden individuals have bloomed within 7-8 years and almost yearly thereafter. The pistillate plants are the most attractive due to the straw-colored fruits which remain on the plants for many months.

USES:*Nolina parryi* is limited in its value for most gardeners but for the native garden or for rocky hillsides it can be used as a very attractive and interesting accent plant.

Nothing is known about the horticultural history of this species.

PHOTOGRAPH BY RALPH C. CORNELL

Nolina parryi

YELLOW BUSH PENSTEMON 5 feet *Penstemon antirrhinoides*

DESCRIPTION: A stiff much-branched upright shrub 3-5 ft. tall (8 ft. in extreme cases) and from 2-5 ft. across; leaves opposite, linear to narrowly elliptical, ¼-¾ in. long, bright green, leaf margins smooth; flowers borne in large leafy much-branched clusters, individual flowers bright lemon-yellow, ½-¾ in. long with a short tube which is abruptly

Penstemon cordifolius

Penstemon antirrhinoides

dilated to form a broadly-gaping 2-lipped flower, the upper lip hooded, the lower one reflexed, buds brownish-red.

FLOWERING: April to June.

DISTRIBUTION: *Penstemon antirrhinoides* is found on dry open slopes from Ontario and Banning south to northern Baja California.

PROPAGATION: This penstemon is easily grown from seed, which, sown in a flat during the fall, germinates within a week or two. The young seedlings should be transplanted to individual containers as soon as they are an inch or so tall. By early spring the plants will be large enough to plant out and they can be expected to bloom that summer. While they prefer a coarse well-drained soil they can be grown in heavy loam or even adobe provided that they are not watered during the summer. They should receive full sun or very light shade.

USES: One objection to this beautiful and most unusual penstemon is that it goes dormant during late summer and loses its leaves, the bushes remaining bare until the rains begin in the winter. For this reason it is a plant of limited use in some gardens. It is, however highly recommended for the native garden and for those who either do not mind the period of leaflessness or who can place the plants where they will be inconspicuous during the period of dormancy.

This species was discovered by Coulter in 1832 and was introduced into cultivation probably in the early 1870's.

HONEYSUCKLE PENSTEMON   4 feet   *Penstemon cordifolius*

DESCRIPTION: A loosely branched shrub with long flexible arching branches often as much as 8 ft. long; leaves fuchsia-like, ovate or oblong-ovate, generally heart-shaped at the base, ½-2 in. long, dark green, margin of leaf set with sharp teeth; flowers borne in dense clusters at the tips of the branches usually more or less on one side of the stem, individual flowers dull scarlet (or yellow), 1-1½ in. long, tubular and strongly 2-lipped.

FLOWERING: April to June; first year plants July and August.

DISTRIBUTION: *Penstemon cordifolius* is found on slopes and in gullies in the chaparral from Santa Barbara County south to Baja California and on San Clemente, Santa Cruz, Santa Rosa and Santa Catalina Islands.

PROPAGATION: This shrub is easily grown from seed which germinates readily when planted during late fall or early spring either in flats or sown directly where the plants are wanted. The seedlings, which tend to be touchy when small, can be transplanted to individual pots when they are large enough to handle and plants from fall-sown seed will bloom during the late spring and summer.

As with most of our native penstemons this species should be provided with a coarse well-drained soil and they should be given little or no water during the summer. While this plant can be grown in full sun it probably does better in partial shade.

USES: When in bloom this is a most attractive species and quite un-penstemon like in appearance. It is admirably suited for growing among other shrubs and can even be used as a bedding plant. For this purpose it is best the first year when it is only about 18-24 in. tall. Older plants if pruned back send up long vigorous shoots which may become 4-5 ft. long in a single season.

One objection to this penstemon is the fact that it goes dormant during late summer and loses most of its leaves. For this reason some people may prefer to use it more as an annual and remove the plants after they have finished blooming.

A yellow-flowered form is also known and the two colors are very attractive when grown together.

Penstemon cordifolius was first collected by Douglas in 1831 but it was not introduced into cultivation until seed was sent to England by Hartweg in 1848.

HOLLY-LEAVED CHERRY   30 feet   *Prunus ilicifolia*

DESCRIPTION: A much-branched evergreen shrub or small tree to 20-30 ft. tall and often nearly equally broad, bark smooth, dark gray, twigs reddish or brown; leaves alternate, rigid, elliptical to oval, either sharp pointed or rounded at the tip, ¾-2 in. long, ¾-1½ in. wide, leaf margins usually wavy and spiny-toothed, mature leaf dark shiny green above, lighter beneath, the entire leaf very holly-like; flowers in slender elongated clusters

Prunus lyonii

125

2-several inches long appearing just before or with the new leaves, individual flowers small, ½ in. or less across, white, with 5 petals; fruit fleshy, 1-seeded, about ¾ in. in diameter, reddish-purple or occasionally yellowish, flesh thin, sweet, stone large.

FLOWERING: March to May or June.

DISTRIBUTION: *Prunus ilicifolia* is found on mountain slopes and in valleys at altitudes from 100-4000 ft. from the Napa Range to the western part of the Tehachapi Mts. and south into Baja California.

PROPAGATION: The Holly-leaved Cherry (also known as Islay, Evergreen Cherry, California Cherry, or Mountain Cherry) is readily grown from seeds which should be gathered as soon as mature. If possible the seeds should be planted in the spot where they are to remain, in which case several seeds are planted together and later all the seedlings removed except one. The seeds can, however, be put in gallon cans. They should never be placed in small pots because the roots quickly become coiled and the plant will never develop a normal root system.

While this shrub will tolerate nearly any soil it grows best in one that is coarse and well-drained. The first season the plants will require some water but after that it needs only moderate irrigation.

USES: The Holly-leaved Cherry is highly recommended for planting in California where it may be used for a number of purposes such as for background planting or for screening. Because of its dense bright green foliage which remains attractive all year it is probably at its best when used as a hedge, either kept in a relatively low clipped form or allowed to become taller and remain unclipped.

The date when the Holly-leaved Cherry was introduced into horticulture is not known. According to one authority the early Spanish settlers used it to decorate their gardens. It was introduced into Europe before 1850 and it is known to have been planted as a hedge in Santa Clara County as early as 1857.

CATALINA CHERRY   45 feet   *Prunus lyonii*

DESCRIPTION: A large evergreen shrub or tree as much as 45 ft. tall and attaining a maximum spread of up to 30 ft. although usually much smaller; leaves alternate, rather egg-shaped, broadest near the base and tapering to a point, 3-5 in. long, leaf margins smooth or faintly toothed when young; flowers borne in dense spikes 4-6 in. long containing 20-40 white flowers, individual flowers about ⅜ in. across with 5-6 petals; fruit ¾-1 in. in diameter, somewhat resembling a large black cherry, usually 1-several fruits on a pendant stalk, flesh thin, rather sweet but with an unpleasant after-taste, stone large.

FLOWERING: March to May or June.

DISTRIBUTION: *Prunus lyonii* occurs only on Santa Catalina, San Clemente, and Santa Cruz Islands where it is common.

PROPAGATION: Propagation of this species is by seeds which should be planted soon after they are ripe. It is best to remove the pulp and sow them where the plants are wanted. If that is impractical they may be placed in boxes of moist sharp sand. The former method is preferable. Germination usually takes place within a few weeks and if the seeds are germinated in sand they should be placed in gallon cans as soon as they are large enough to handle. Another method is to put the seeds in gallon cans thus avoiding the necessity of transplanting the seedlings when they are small.

The plants can be set into their permanent locations at nearly any season of the year although early spring is probably the best. They are not particular as to soil type, water, or exposure and have few diseases or insect pests.

Prunus lyonii flowers

Prunus lyonii fruit

USES: The Catalina Cherry with its abundance of bright green foliage is attractive the entire year and is highly recommended for use as a specimen tree for the garden, as small street trees, and for both clipped and unclipped hedges. The one single objection to this species is that it is messy when the fruit drops. This is especially serious where the plants are used for street plantings.

The Catalina Cherry has long been used as a garden subject in California and is available at most nurseries. *Prunus lyonii* hybridizes readily with *Prunus ilicifolia*, the Holly-leaved Cherry, when the two are grown together and many of the plants seen in California today are hybrids between the two species.

BUCKTHORN   5 feet   *Rhamnus crocea*

DESCRIPTION: A low much-branched evergreen shrub up to 5 ft. tall, bark on old branches gray, often quite dark, on young branches reddish or reddish-purple; leaves either scattered on the branches or fascicled on short spur branches, elliptic to nearly round, ½-1 in. long, hard, leathery, green above, yellowish-brown below, margins set with small teeth each ending in a small gland or the margins may be nearly smooth; flowers in small clusters in the axils of the leaves, individual flowers small, yellowish-green, the staminate and pistillate flowers borne on separate plants; fruit a nearly round shining red berry about ¼ in. long.

FLOWERING: February to May; fruit June to September.

DISTRIBUTION: *Rhamus crocea* is found near the coast from western Lake County south to San Diego County and on into Baja California.

PROPAGATION: Buckthorn is easily propagated by seeds which germinate readily when fresh. For older seeds Mirov and Kraebel recommend 3-months stratification. The young plants should be transplanted from the seed flats to individual containers when they are large enough to handle.

In the garden Buckthorn should be given a coarse, well-drained soil with little or no water during the summer months, the latter point is especially important if the soil tends to be heavy.

USES: While the flowers are more or less unimportant the plant is extremely attractive during late summer when it is covered with the bright red berries. It must be remembered however, that only the pistillate individuals bear fruit so in order to produce the colorful red berries, staminate plants must be included in the garden.

Rhamnus crocea tolerates trimming very well and it can be kept as a low clipped hedge.

According to Sargent, Hartweg first introduced *Rhamnus crocea* into cultivation in England in 1846. The Royal Horticultural Society's "Dictionary of Gardening" gives 1848 as its date of introduction.

LEMONADE BERRY   10 feet   *Rhus integrifolia*

DESCRIPTION: A medium to large evergreen shrub 3-10 ft. tall, sometimes even a small tree up to 25 ft.; leaves alternate, elliptical to nearly round, 1-2½ in. long, ¾-1½ in. wide usually blunt on either end, thick, leathery, dull green above and lighter below, margins somewhat wavy and either smooth or irregularly toothed; flowers borne in terminal clusters of 25-40 flowers, individual flowers small, about ¼ in. across, with 5 white or pinkish petals; fruit rounded and somewhat flattened, usually covered with a waxy secretion, reddish at maturity.

FLOWERING: February and March.

DISTRIBUTION: *Rhus integrifolia* is found on bluffs and mesas along the coast of southern California from Santa Barbara County south into Baja California but it does not occur very far inland. It is also known from several of the islands lying off the coast of California.

PROPAGATION: Lemonade Berry is propagated by seeds which are best planted in the autumn in outside seedbeds or in flats. To hasten germination these seeds should first be soaked overnight in water which has been heated to 180°F. In two or three months the seedlings will be large enough to transplant to individual containers and they will often be large enough to set out the first spring in which case they will usually do better than if they were held until the following spring. During the first season plants should receive careful attention until they have become established. The Lemonade Berry thrives in nearly any soil or habitat, however, they do best near the coast and for areas farther inland another species, *R. ovata* is recommended.

USES: Lemonade Berry has been used as a garden plant for a long time and in some ways is a more satisfactory subject than the two following species, since it readily adapts itself to ordinary garden care. One objection some people may have to it is that the leaves are rather gray-green in color and from a distance the plants look as though they were covered with dust.

Rhus integrifolia makes an excellent low clipped hedge and has the advantage of holding its leaves all the way to the ground, a very important feature in selecting material for use as hedges. It can also be used as a low clipped ground cover for banks, etc.

It is not known when this shrub was first brought into cultivation.

LAUREL SUMAC   20 feet   *Rhus laurina*

DESCRIPTION: An evergreen shrub 10-20 ft. tall usually forming a dense rounded mound; leaves alternate, egg-shaped to lance-like, 2-4 in. long, ¾-1½ in. wide, leathery, dark green above, lighter below, reddish when young, margins smooth; flowers borne in dense terminal clusters often 6-8 in. long and 4-5 in. wide at the base containing hundreds of small flowers, buds purplish-red and opening to a creamy-white, flowers either male or female and borne on separate plants; fruit small, about ⅛ in. in diameter, whitish, containing a single seed.

FLOWERING: May to July.

DISTRIBUTION: *Rhus laurina* is found near the coast from Santa Barbara County south to Baja California but never very far inland. It is also known from San Clemente, Santa Catalina, and Cedrus Islands.

PROPAGATION: *Rhus laurina* is grown from seeds which should be planted in the fall or early spring. Good results are obtained by growing the seedlings in 4-in. pots the first summer and planting them out late that fall or early winter. The Laurel Sumac is not particular as to soil and good drainage is not essential; however, if it is grown in heavy adobe water should be withheld during the summer. The plants develop best when grown in full sun and in rich soil growth is rapid.

The Laurel Sumac is more sensitive to frost than are most of the native shrubs and even at the Rancho Santa Ana Botanic Garden's location in Orange County where they are native on the dry hillsides, they are sometimes frosted during the winter.

USES: *Rhus laurina* is not as desirable for ornamental purposes as either *Rhus integrifolia* or *Rhus ovata* except that it is a more rapid grower and in some coastal regions seems to thrive under more trying conditions than either of the other two.

Nothing is known about its horticultural history.

SUGARBUSH   12 feet   *Rhus ovata*

DESCRIPTION: A compact well-rounded evergreen shrub as much as 12 ft. high; leaves egg-shaped, tapering to a point, 1½-4 in. long, ¾-1½ in. wide, thick, leathery, deep green above, lighter below, margins smooth or rarely with small teeth, the sides of the leaf fold upward from the midvein making them trough-like; flowers borne in dense terminal cone-shaped clusters 2-3 in. long, individual flowers small, about 3/16 in. across, creamy with tinges of red; fruit small, rounded and flattened, covered with a sugary or waxy secretion, mahogany-red at maturity.

Rhus ovata

FLOWERING: March to May.

DISTRIBUTION: *Rhus ovata* is found in southern California on chaparral slopes inland a short distance from the coast from Santa Barbara County south to San Diego County and east to the edge of the desert. It is known also from Santa Catalina and Santa Cruz Islands.

PROPAGATION: Sugarbush is propagated by seeds which should be planted soon after gathering. The pulp should be removed and the seeds soaked for 24-48 hours in water which has been heated to 180-200°F. They may then be sown in flats or outdoor seedbeds.

130

Rhus ovata fruit

Rhus ovata flowers

Because the plants have a long taproot, it is better to put the young seedlings directly into a large can rather than first into small pots. With careful handling the species can be transplanted bare-root in January directly from the seedbeds. If only a few plants are needed it is probably advisable to buy them in gallon cans from a nursery as the seedlings are slow growing and require nearly a year to become large enough for planting.

The Sugarbush does best in full sun and with good drainage but will grow in a variety of soils. Experience at the Rancho Santa Ana Botanic Garden has been that in general this species will not tolerate much summer watering. There are, however, some conspicuous exceptions. One large specimen has been growing for a number of years in a plot planted with Beach Strawberry *(Fragaria chiloensis)* which has been irrigated rather regularly during the summer months. Another example, and even more striking, is at Mills College in Oakland where a plant set in a low wet situation in 1926 is still growing and in 1948 was 18 ft. high with a spread of over 27 ft. McMinn concludes that this plant's adaptability to soil moisture and soil texture is remarkable.

USES: Sugarbush is one of the most desirable of all the native shrubs as it is attractive all year and is not troubled to any degree by insect pests or disease. The flower clusters are formed during late fall and the reddish buds add to the attractiveness of the plant during the winter. Because of its compact habit it is recommended for screens and background plantings as well as for specimen shrubs. It is also highly desirable for roadside plantings and for banks.

The date of its introduction into horticulture is not known.

FLOWERING CURRANT   8 feet   *Ribes sanguineum*

DISTRIBUTION: An erect or spreading deciduous shrub 4-8 ft. tall, lacking spines; leaves alternate, 3-5-lobed, 1-2 in. broad, margins of leaf irregularly toothed; flowers borne in elongated clusters of 10 or more flowers, clusters usually held erect, individual flower with a funnel-shaped calyx-tube, 1/8-3/16 in. long, commonly pubescent with short-stalked glandular hairs, calyx-lobes spreading, petals white or pink or even blood-red, shorter than the calyx-lobes; fruit a roundish berry ¼-⅜ in. long, blue-black with a whitish bloom.

FLOWERING: March to June.

DISTRIBUTION: *Ribes sanguineum* is found on moist slopes in the Coast Ranges at altitudes of 2000-6000 ft. from British Columbia south to Lake, Marin, and Santa Clara counties.

PROPAGATION: The Flowering Currant is easily grown from seed sown in flats or in outdoor seedbeds and later transplanted. It can also be propagated from cuttings and this method is recommended for maintaining especially fine forms of this species. Since the untreated seed may be quite slow to germinate, Mirov recommends that it be stratified for 3 months. The young plants are best grown in a lath house the first season and set out during the following fall and winter. In the garden they should, if possible, be given a light soil containing considerable leafmold and in southern California they should be given partial shade.

USES: As with nearly all the native currants and gooseberries, the Flowering Currant loses its leaves and becomes dormant for a period in late summer and early fall. It should, therefore, be placed where it will not be unsightly during the period when it is leafless. With the first fall rains the plants begin growth and they may be in bloom as early as December. *Ribes sanguineum* has been a garden favorite in many parts of the country for years and numerous horticultural forms have been developed, these differing usually only in flower color or in the size of the flower cluster. One of the finest of these is *Ribes sanguineum* var. *splendens,* a form with blood-red flowers. Double-flowered forms have been reported as has a yellow-leafed form.

In the southern part of the state *Ribes sanguineum* is often grown with some difficulty and the variety *glutinosum* is probably a more satisfactory plant than the species. *Ribes sanguineum* var. *glutinosum* differs from the species mainly in having drooping rather than upright flower clusters and the flowers are usually lighter in color. The leaves also tend to be more glandular than they are in the species. This variety is found on moist canyon slopes along the coast from the Smith River in Del Norte County south to San Luis Obispo County.

Ribes sanguineum var. *glutinosum*

Ribes sanguineum was collected by Menzies on his first voyage in 1787 and again in 1792 when he was with the Vancouver Expedition. According to Rehder, it was brought into cultivation in 1818. Douglas introduced it into England in 1826 and it bloomed there for the first time in 1828. This plant was so well received in England that the botanist Lindley wrote " . . . that if the expense incurred by the Horticultural Society in Mr. Douglas's voyage had been attended with no other result than the introduction of this species, there would have been no ground for dissatisfaction."

FUCHSIA-FLOWERED GOOSEBERRY 6 feet *Ribes speciosum*

DESCRIPTION: A deciduous to nearly evergreen shrub 4-6 ft. tall, young stems bristly, spines stout, older stems often nearly smooth; leaves alternate, often in dense clusters along the stem, ½-1 in. long, roundish, 3-5-lobed, base of leaf wedge-shaped, leaves leathery, smooth, dark glossy green above, lighter beneath; flowers in clusters of 1-4 on slender stems hanging from arched branches; flowers deep crimson with long-projecting stamens, the flowers somewhat resembling those of the fuchsia; berry about ½ in. long, dry and glandular-bristly.

FLOWERING: January to April.

DISTRIBUTION: *Ribes speciosum* is found in the chaparral and oak belts at elevations of 2000 ft. or less from Monterey and Santa Clara counties south along the coast to San Diego County.

PROPAGATION: The Fuchsia-Flowered Gooseberry is easily propagated by seed or by cuttings taken in the fall. Seed sown in flats germinates quickly and the seedlings may be potted when large enough to handle. The young plants are best held in the lath house the first season and planted out the following autumn. They are not particular as to soil but grow best in a well-drained site in partial shade. The first season they should be watered but after that time summer irrigation should be avoided. Pruning should be confined to the removal of old and straggly canes which will then encourage vigorous new shoots.

USES: *Ribes speciosum* has been listed by McMinn as one of the ten best native shrubs. Certainly when it is in flower, with every branch thickly hung with deep crimson flowers, it is one of the most spectacular of the native shrubs. In the garden it can be used in mixed plantings, as a filler, or as a specimen plant. If used as a specimen plant it must be remembered that it is leafless during late summer and therefore its placement must be carefully

Ribes speciosum

considered. It is especially attractive on banks where the flowers may be viewed from below.

This species was first collected by Menzies while he was with the Vancouver Expedition and it was brought into cultivation in 1828 from seed collected by Collie, surgeon with the Beechey Expedition. David Douglas in writing about this plant said that is was "a flower not surpassed in beauty by the finest Fuchsia."

Ribes viburnifolium

VIBURNUM-LEAVED CURRANT   3 feet   *Ribes viburnifolium*

DESCRIPTION: A straggling evergreen shrub usually less than 3 ft. tall but often spreading as much as 5 ft.; leaves alternate, roundish to oval, up to 1½ in. long, tough and leathery, dark green above, lower side lighter and covered with resinous dots, margins smooth or nearly so, leaves fragrant; flowers in few-to-several flowered clusters, individual blooms small and rather inconspicuous but produced in such quantities that they give the entire plant a reddish cast; berry oval, about ¼ in. long, red when ripe.

FLOWERING: February to April.

DISTRIBUTION: *Ribes viburnifolium* was first collected at Todos Santos Bay, Baja California; in California it is known only from Santa Catalina Island where it is found in moist places on the sides of canyons.

PROPAGATION: The Viburnum-Leaved Currant is easily propagated from seeds or by either soft or hardwood cuttings. Seed may be sown in flats and the young seedlings later potted when they are large enough to handle. They are best held in containers the first season and then planted out the following fall or winter. In the garden the plants are not

135

particular as to soil but if they are grown in heavy clay loams they should be given very little summer watering. In the coastal areas this currant can be grown in full sun but in the hotter inland areas it requires light shade otherwise the leaves either burn or become yellowish during the summer months. Occasionally plants send up straight upright stems, these should be removed in order to maintain the low spreading form of the plant.

USES: Few of the native low-growing evergreen shrubs are more satisfactory for use in gardens than this very un-currant-like currant. In the garden it is especially useful and attractive planted along banks or walls or in places where a low-growing shrub is needed. Since this species is evergreen it is one currant that is attractive all year. It can also be used as a ground cover in areas where there is some shade.

This species is so unlike the other Ribes that the early collectors did not even recognize it as one. It was first grown in England from seed received in 1897 from Harvard University which in turn had received it from Santa Catalina Island, very possibly from Mrs. Trask. Mrs. Trask, who was an early resident on the island, wrote about it saying that it "thrives in all parts of the island in moist places" and that one canyon "is clothed with this beautiful Ribes—mile after mile of overhanging rocks being festooned with its branches."

Another species of Ribes which is sometimes grown as an ornamental is *Ribes aureum,* the Golden Currant. It is a deciduous shrub 4-8 ft. tall with smooth leaves ½-1 in. broad, usually 3-5-lobed. The yellow flowers are borne in long drooping clusters and these are followed by yellow, red or black berries. This species is found in moist situations over a large area east of the Sierra Nevada, from Inyo to Siskiyou County, north to British Columbia, and east to the Rocky Mts. The variety *gracillimum* is similar to the species differing mainly in being scentless. It is found in coastal areas from Contra Costa County south to Riverside.

MATILIJA POPPY   8 feet   *Romneya coulteri*

DESCRIPTION: A vigorous woody-based perennial with wand-like stems as much as 8 ft. tall; stems and leaves gray-green, smooth except for a few weak spines on the petioles and margins of the leaves; leaves alternate, 3-4 in. long and equally broad, deeply cut into 3-5 major lobes, these in turn often irregularly cut into narrow lobes; flowers borne singly at the tips of the branches, often forming a several-flowered cluster, flowers large, from 4-9 in. in diameter, white, fragrant, usually 6-petaled, the petals having the appearance of white tissue paper which has been crumpled and then spread out, stamens numerous, forming a yellow cluster at the center of the flower; seed capsule 1-2 in. long, tapering at both ends, seeds black, numerous.

FLOWERING: June and July.

DISTRIBUTION: *Romneya coulteri* inhabits washes and canyon beds at altitudes of 1000-2000 ft. in coastal California from Santa Barbara County south to San Diego County and Baja California.

PROPAGATION: The Matilija Poppy is easily propagated by suckers removed from older plants or by root cuttings. While root cuttings have never been attempted at this botanic garden, the Santa Barbara Botanic Garden has successfully used this method for a number of years. They recommend taking sections of young lateral roots about the diameter of a lead pencil in November or December. These are cut into sections about 2½ in. long. As a rooting mixture they use 2/5 loam, 1/5 sand, 1/5 peat, and 1/5 leafmold. This material is placed in a six-inch pot or in gallon cans and a small pocket is made of pure sand into which the cutting is placed in a horizontal position. The containers are then watered lightly each day. Young shoots should appear in about 30 days.

The Matilija Poppy can also be grown from seed, but this is often difficult because the seedlings are very susceptible to damping-off and they are often not easily transplanted.

Romneya coulteri (left) ; *Romneya* 'White Cloud' (right)

The most successful germination was obtained at the Rancho Santa Ana Botanic Garden by planting the seed in flats and then burning straw or pine needles over the flat.

While the plants thrive best in a light coarse soil, they will grow in heavy loams but it is imperative that they have good drainage as they will not tolerate a poorly drained wet position. However, if given a little water during the summer, they will remain more attractive than they otherwise would. The plants should have an exposure of full sun.

USES: The Matilija Poppy is certainly one of the most spectacular of all the plants native to California, and in Europe it has been said that this is the most beautiful ornamental to come out of California. It, however, cannot be recommended for the small garden because of its size and also because of its cultural requirements. For larger gardens where there is room for it to grow to full size, and for native gardens, it is highly recommended. When the plants become unsightly, they should be cut back nearly to the ground and they will then send up vigorous new growth.

The Matilija Poppy was first introduced into England by E. G. Henderson and Son about 1875 and has been popular wherever it has proven hardy. It has been offered for sale in California at least since 1911.

Romneya trichocalyx is another species which is sometimes grown. It differs from *R. coulteri* botanically in having sepals which are beakless but covered with short bristle-like hairs while *R. coulteri* has sepals which are slightly beaked and free from hairs. Too, the petals of *R. trichocalyx* look as though they had been pleated lengthwise whereas those of *R. coulteri* look more nearly as though they had been crumpled and then straightened out. Horticulturally *coulteri* has been considered the better species. Hybrids between the two have been grown and a variety called 'White Cloud,' which is now sold by some nurserymen, may be of hybrid origin.

137

CLEVELAND'S SAGE   4 feet   *Salvia clevelandii*

DESCRIPTION: A low rounded shrub 3-4 ft. high with very aromatic foliage; leaves opposite, oblong to lanceolate-oblong, ¾-1½ in. long, gray-green above, leaf margins smooth or set with fine rounded teeth; flowers in heads either solitary or set far apart on the stems, flowers vivid blue or violet-blue in color, tubular, 2-lipped about ¾ in. long.

FLOWERING: May to August.

DISTRIBUTION: *Salvia clevelandii* is found on chaparral slopes in middle and western San Diego County.

PROPAGATION: This salvia is readily propagated by seed sown in flats during the fall or winter. When large enough to handle, the young seedlings should be transplanted to pots and later set out into their permanent locations. Ordinarily the plants will not bloom the first year. In the garden they should be given a sunny location in well-drained soil and no water during the summer. The plants may be kept more attractive if the flower-stalks are removed after they are no longer desirable and this trimming will induce more abundant flowering the following year.

USES: *Salvia clevelandii* produces its brilliant blue flowers (an albino form is known also) after a great many of the native plants have finished blooming. It has been grown at This Garden since 1930 and is considered the most attractive of the sages. One of the delightful things about this shrub is its fragrance which is unmistakable. Unfortunately, Cleveland's Sage cannot be recommended to the average gardener due to its cultural requirements but for native gardens, dry banks, and hillsides it is a very beautiful and useful plant.

PURPLE SAGE   5 feet   *Salvia leucophylla*

DESCRIPTION: An aromatic gray-leaved evergreen shrub 3-5 ft. high and equally broad, bark on old stems gray, young growth reddish or purplish-green; leaves opposite, oblong-lanceolate, 2-3 in. long, gray-green or gray above, gray and hairy on the under side, margins of leaf set with small round teeth, flowers borne in whorls spaced along the upper part of the stem, individual flowers 2-lipped, about ¾ in. long, purplish-lavender or pinkish.

FLOWERING: May and June.

DISTRIBUTION: *Salvia leucophylla* is found on dry slopes in the mountains along the coast from San Luis Obispo County south to Orange County.

PROPAGATION: Purple Sage is propagated by seeds which germinate within a few days. The seedlings can be planted in individual pots as soon as they are large enough to handle and plants from fall-sown seed may then be put in the garden the following spring. This species is useful because it will grow in heavy soil and is apparently improved by a small amount of water during the summer.

USES: Purple Sage is a well-known southern California native but like the other sages it cannot be recommended to the average gardener. In the native garden, however, it can be used to advantage as a rather large, gray-leaved plant desirable for background plantings; and Lester Rowntree suggests combining it with Matilija Poppy. She also suggests some pruning when young in order to develop well-shaped plants. It will also look less untidy late in the season if the old flower-stalks are removed after the blooming season. This species is also useful for covering dry slopes and banks.

Nothing is known about horticultural history of this plant.

Salvia clevelandii and *S. leucophylla* hybridize readily and plants of this cross have been grown at the Botanic Garden under the name Salvia 'Allen Chickering.'

138

Salvia clevelandii

PHOTOGRAPH BY DOUGLAS EBERSOLE

Styrax officinalis var. *californica*

SNOW-DROP BUSH   8 feet   *Styrax officinalis* var. *californica*

DESCRIPTION: An erect deciduous shrub 3-8 ft. high; leaves alternate, round-ovate, oval or egg-shaped, 1-3½ in. long, 1-nerved from the base; flowers pendulous in small terminal clusters, white, fragrant, somewhat resembling orange blossoms, petals 4-8, commonly 6, ½-1 in. long, united at the base; fruit globose, about ½ in. in diameter.

FLOWERING: April to June.

DISTRIBUTION: *Styrax officinalis* var. *californica* occurs on dry slopes in the foothills from Lake County to Tehama County and in the Sierra Nevada foothills from Shasta County south to Tulare County. It is also found in the San Bernardino and Santa Ana Mts.

PROPAGATION: This species is somewhat difficult to propagate. Seeds sown in flats germinate within a month or so and it is during the seedling stage that they are so difficult to maintain, since they are quite susceptible to damping-off and any excess water may cause the entire lot of seedlings to be lost within a few days. When large enough to handle, the plants can be transferred to individual pots containing a gritty soil mixture.

In the garden they should be placed in partial shade in a coarse, well-drained soil. When once established, they will thrive without summer irrigation but they will remain more attractive if they are given a small amount of water from time to time.

USES: The Snow-Drop Bush is a most attractive shrub when in bloom and it should be placed where the lovely white pendent flowers can be enjoyed when they are present. It is, however, deciduous and some gardeners may object to it for that reason. Too, it has a very short blooming period. This species is probably best used in a mixed planting where it will receive partial shade from larger shrubs and in such a location the branches which are bare during the winter will not be at all objectionable. In early spring the fresh young leaves followed shortly by the attractive white flowers make the plant a most valuable addition to any mixed planting of native trees and shrubs.

Trichostema lanatum

WOOLLY BLUE CURLS   5 feet   *Trichostema lanatum*

DESCRIPTION: An erect aromatic, much-branched evergreen shrub 3-5 ft. tall; leaves opposite, 1¼-2 in. long, narrow, shiny green above, white hairy below, margins of leaf rolled under, fascicles of smaller leaves borne in the axils of the larger leaves; inflorescence long and narrow, made up of small clusters of from 4-12 flowers each, branches of inflorescence and external flower parts covered with dense purple, blue, or white wool, the unopened flowers consist of a tube about ¼ in. long at the tip of which is a rounded ball about ¼ in. in diameter which on opening becomes a 5-parted corolla, 4 of the corolla lobes being alike and the fifth larger and usually white spotted.

FLOWERING: April and May; in cultivation much longer.

DISTRIBUTION: *Trichostema lanatum* is found occasionally on dry slopes and along the coast from San Benito and Monterey counties south to San Diego County and inland as far as Mint Canyon and the Santa Ana Mts.

PROPAGATION: Woolly Blue Curls can be grown either from seed or cuttings. Since the seeds are slow in germinating, Mirov recommends that they be stratified for three months at 32°F. The same author also recommends the use of old stored seed rather than fresh seed. Usually, however, even at the best, germination is poor.

Heel cutting may be rooted in the cold frame and this method is recommended where it is desired to maintain an especially fine form. In the garden their success depends upon a well-drained light soil. It is also important that the soil is not very rich and finally the plants should not receive irrigation during the summer. In areas where they thrive they will volunteer quite readily.

Trichostema lanatum flowers

USES: Woolly Blue Curls is an unusual shrub that supplies a color which is all too rare among our native plants and for this reason it is recommended to gardeners. While it is not the easiest of the natives to grow it can be maintained fairly well if it is placed in a location away from summer watering. Since the plants are fairly small and do not take a great deal of space, there is often a dry bank or corner in the garden where they can be grown quite successfully.

Woolly Blue Curls was first collected by Douglas, but the species was not introduced into cultivation until recent times.

142

MOJAVE YUCCA 5-15 feet when in flower *Yucca schidigera*

DESCRIPTION: An evergreen shrub 5 to as much as 15 ft. high with from one to several trunks which may be up to 1 ft. in diameter with the lower portion devoid of the old dead leaves; leaves 2-3 ft. long and 1-2 in. wide, olive or yellowish-green, rarely bluish, nearly straight and at first erect but later becoming deflexed, each leaf tipped with a sharp spine, margins of leaf bearing long thread-like fibers; inflorescence a large panicle often over 2 ft. long and 1 ft. wide containing several hundred flowers; individual flowers large, composed of six segments 1½-2¾ in. long, the outer three greenish-brown on the outside and creamy inside, the inner three creamy white on both surfaces; fruit dull brown or tan, 2½-2¾ in. long containing numerous flattened black seeds.

FLOWERING: March and April.

DISTRIBUTION: *Yucca schidigera* is found on dry slopes and mesas in the Mojave and Colorado deserts, south into Baja California, west into San Diego County and east to Nevada and Arizona.

PROPAGATION: The Mojave Yucca is propagated by seed which germinates readily when sown either in flats or in outdoor seedbeds. The plants can remain in the seedbed for the first year and then be moved to gallon cans and grown a second year, at the end of which time they will be ready to plant out. In order to avoid crown-rot while in the nursery, it is very important that the crown should not be covered with soil when the plants are potted.

In the garden the yucca should have a well-drained coarse soil and should be watered only the first year, after this time it will grow without special care. Overhead irrigation should be avoided since it probably favors crown-rot. At the Rancho Santa Ana Botanic Garden plants of this species have bloomed within eight years.

USES: This species has very limited value as a subject for most gardens and should not be attempted at all in small gardens. It can, however, be recommended for large native plantings or for dry banks and hillsides or for desert areas.

Often listed under the name *Yucca mohavensis*, it is correctly termed *Yucca schidigera*.

OUR LORD'S CANDLE 5-14 feet when in flower *Yucca whipplei*

DESCRIPTION: An apparently stemless plant with the leaves borne in a dense basal rosette either solitary or forming small to large clumps with numerous rosettes, leaves grayish-green, 8-20 in. long, narrow, rigid and tipped with a slender spine; inflorescence 5-14 ft. tall in overall length, the large terminal flower cluster containing numerous large pendent flowers, which vary in size from 1½-2½ in. long, creamy and often with purplish markings on the outside of the outer 3 segment; fruit a capsule about 1¼ in. long containing numerous flattened black seeds.

FLOWERING: April through June.

DISTRIBUTION: *Yucca whipplei* is common on dry slopes and mesas in southern California extending north to Monterey and San Benito counties.

PROPAGATION: This species is propagated by seed which should be planted either in outdoor seedbeds or in extra deep flats. The seedlings can be allowed to grow the first year without transplanting and then be put bareroot directly into their permanent locations the second year. They should be given careful attention the first year after they are set out but after that will grow without special care, requiring no more water than they receive from natural rainfall. Flowering will commence in from 4-8 years depending upon environmental conditions. After blooming the plants which have only a solitary rosette of

143

leaves will die but those which produce side shoots will continue to grow with only the rosette that has bloomed dying. In the garden the plants should be given a coarse rocky soil.

USES: As with the preceding species, this yucca has limited value in most gardens but for dry rocky hills and slopes which can be cared for only with difficulty or for native gardens this species is highly recommended as one of the most spectacular of our native plants. During the spring months the towering clusters of flowers of this species are one of the most imposing sights to be seen on the dry foothills of southern California's coastal and desert districts.

Yucca whipplei

4. Trees

In a flora well known for the number of species which it has contributed to ornamental horticulture, no group is better represented than are the trees of California. Not only have many of the species become common in gardens in many parts of the world but a number of them have also become almost as well known through the work of artists, photographers and writers.

The evergreens have been especially popular from early times and a number of horticultural expeditions sent to California had as a prime objective the introduction of these handsome trees. An interesting example of what has happened to some of these species after their introduction into cultivation may be seen in the horticultural history of the Lawson Cypress *(Chamaecyparis lawsoniana)*. Native to the moist hillsides and canyon bottoms of northwestern California and southwestern Oregon the Lawson Cypress was introduced into cultivation by Peter Lawson and Co. of Edinburgh from seed sent from California by Wm. Murray in 1853. Under garden cultivation this plant has produced a very large number of sports many of which have been named and propagated. At the present time there are some eighty horticulturally distinct varieties of this species.

Because many of the native trees are so well known and so much has already been written about them, it is thought best to discuss here only a few species which, while they thrive and do well in southern California, are not as well known nor as widely grown as they should be.

INCENSE CEDAR 150 feet *Libocedrus decurrens*

DESCRIPTION: An evergreen tree as much as 150 feet tall in the forest, young trees narrow-pyramidal in shape with branches to the ground, mature trees somewhat irregular, bark on young trees and branches broken into reddish-brown plates, branchlets alternate, arranged in flat slightly drooping sprays which are arranged vertically rather than horizontally, foliage dark glossy green on both sides, leaves scale-like, opposite, arranged in 4 rows; staminate and pistillate cones borne on same tree, solitary at the tips of the branchlets, staminate cones ⅛-¼ in. long, pistillate cones pendulous, dark brown, about 1 in. long, ⅜ in. wide, maturing the first year.

DISTRIBUTION: *Libocedrus decurrens* is widely distributed from Oregon south through the Coast Ranges and the Sierra Nevada to the higher mountains of southern California and Baja California.

PROPAGATION: The Incense Cedar is propagated either from seeds or cuttings. Seed may be planted in outdoor seedbeds or in flats in late fall or early spring. The young seedlings should be placed in individual containers when they are 2-3 in. tall and then planted out at the end of the first growing season or they may be lined out and grown in the nursery for several seasons.

Propagation by cuttings, which should be taken in the fall, is recommended if distinctive forms are to be perpetuated.

The regions where the Incense Cedar grows naturally have an annual rainfall of anywhere from 15-50 in., much of it coming during the winter months. Thus the trees are usually subjected to long dry summers making them admirably suited for southern California plantings. In this state the Incense Cedar appears to do equally well in either the coastal regions or in the interior valleys.

USES: *Libocedrus decurrens* is highly recommended for use in California gardens, roadsides, etc. since it seems to be able to thrive under such diverse conditions of soil, moisture and exposure. Because of its relatively narrow growth habit it can be recommended for gardens where many other trees such as the Deodar Cedar are unsuitable because of their more spreading habit.

Lithocarpus densiflora

Numerous horticultural forms of this species are known, most of them, however, being grown only in Europe.

The Incense Cedar was introduced into cultivation in 1853 from seed collected by John Jeffrey for the Oregon Association of Edinburgh.

TAN OAK

150 feet *Lithocarpus densiflora*

DESCRIPTION: An evergreen tree as much as 150 ft. tall; leaves 2½-4½ in. long, 1-1¾ in. wide, oblong, strongly parallel-veined on the under surface with the nerves ending in teeth on the leaf-margins, young leaves rusty-pubescent becoming smooth and whitish in age; flowers small, pistillate flowers borne at the base of the staminate spike; fruit a nut enclosed at the base in a shallow cup similar to the way oak acorns are borne.

DISTRIBUTION: *Lithocarpus densiflora* is found on fertile mountain slopes and ridges from the Santa Ynez Mts. north to Siskiyou County and south along the Sierra Nevada to Mariposa County.

PROPAGATION: The Tan Oak is propagated by seeds which germinate quickly when fresh. They may be sown in flats containing a light soil mixture or peat moss and the young seedlings then may be potted into individual containers after they have germinated.

In the garden the plants should be given some water during the summer and it is important that they be situated so that they will have protection against hot winds. Otherwise the leaves may burn during very hot dry spells. This species does best in the coastal areas and it should not be planted in the interior valleys.

In order to develop dense well-branched trees the young plants should be carefully pruned while they are young. The Tan Oak is a very attractive tree which can be highly recommended for the cooler coastal regions.

According to Rehder this species was introduced into cultivation in 1874.

SANTA CRUZ ISLAND IRON-WOOD

70 feet *Lyonothamnus floribundus* var. *asplenifolius*

DESCRIPTION: A slender evergreen tree as much as 50-70 ft. tall with a single trunk or with a number of stems arising from the ground making it shrub-like, bark thin, reddish-brown, exfoliating in long narrow strips, young twigs covered with fine hairs which later disappear leaving the branchlets bright red; leaves variable but in the variety *asplenifolius* they are very fern-like, each leaf being divided into from 2-7 smaller leaflets each of which is cut into more or less triangular lobes, the entire leaf being from 4-8 in. long and about 4 in. wide, upper surface of leaf smooth, dark green and shiny, underside yellowish-green and rather hairy; flowers borne in large flat-topped clusters 4-8 in. across, individual flowers ⅛-¼ in. in diameter, white, with an odor which many people find unpleasant; fruit a woody capsule usually containing 4 seeds.

FLOWERING: June and July.

DISTRIBUTION: *Lyonothamnus floribundus* var. *asplenifolius* is found on Santa Catalina, San Clemente, Santa Cruz, and Santa Rosa Islands where it grows in dry rocky soil on steep canyon slopes.

PROPAGATION: The Santa Cruz Island Iron-Wood is propagated by seed which germinates in about two weeks. Seedlings should be transplanted from the flats to small pots and later put into gallon cans in which they can be grown until they are ready for setting out into the garden. The plants will grow in a wide variety of soils as long as there is good drainage. They are best in coastal areas and should not be planted in the hot inland valleys.

The Santa Cruz Island Iron-Wood is one of the most striking and unusual trees found in California and it is highly recommended for planting in the warmer coastal areas of the state where it may be used as a specimen tree or for street or roadside plantings. It is a rapid grower and stands pruning well.

147

Lyonothamnus floribundus var. *asplenifolius*

This most desirable tree was first discovered on Santa Catalina in 1884 by W. S. Lyon, California's first State Forester. There are, however, unconfirmed reports that it had been collected earlier. H. C. Ford reports hearing of this "Iron-Wood" as early as 1875 and he tried "to procure specimens at the hands of sailors and others frequenting the island." It was, however, first introduced into cultivation by Dr. Franceschi in 1894 from plants growing on Santa Cruz Island. Franceschi recommended it for street planting in southern California and listed it in the catalogue of the Southern California Acclimatizing Association in 1908 at $1.00 for plants in 2½-in. pots. It was introduced into England in 1900 but has proven too tender for general planting there.

Lyonothamnus floribundus which is found only on Catalina Island is similar to the above except that the leaves are 3-6 in. long and they are not cut into leaflets as in the var. *asplenifolius*. There is, however, great variation in this respect and leaves will be found varying all the way from the uncut leaves of species to the very fern-like leaves of *asplenifolius*.

CALIFORNIA NUTMEG   50 feet   *Torreya californica*

DESCRIPTION: An evergreen tree 15-50 ft. or more tall, branches more or less horizontal, often whorled, branchlets pendulous, leaves 1½-3 in. long, about ⅛ in. wide, rigid and tipped with a sharp spine, dark glossy green above, yellowish-green beneath; staminate cones about ⅓ in. long, pistillate cones about ¼ in. long developing into an olive-like fruit

148

approximately 1½ in. long, green later stripped purple, in cross-section similar in appearance to a nutmeg hence the common name.

DISTRIBUTION: *Torreya californica* is found in cool shady canyons from the Santa Cruz Mts. north to Mendocino County and south in the Sierra Nevada as far as Tulare County. Nowhere is it a common forest tree.

PROPAGATION: The California Nutmeg is propagated from seeds. Sown in flats a few seed will germinate the first season but most of them will not come up until the second year. According to the United States Department of Agriculture Woody-Plant Seed Manual it is not certain whether or not stratification is necessary and they report Torreya seeds germinating without stratification but very slowly.

Torreya californica

In the garden the California Nutmeg requires summer waterings and while it grows best in partial shade in an acid soil it has grown at this Botanic Garden in heavy soil which tends to be alkaline. This tree is recommended to gardeners as an unusual and slow-growing evergreen with handsome dark green foliage. The growing of this plant should not be attempted in the hot interior valleys.

Torreya californica was introduced into cultivation in 1851.

149

5. Vines

Compared with the richness of the California flora in species of annuals, shrubs and trees, the state is very wanting when it comes to vines, there being but five species which are of interest to gardeners, three of them for their attractive or unusual flowers, and two of them for their shade-producing leaves.

Aristolochia californica

CALIFORNIA DUTCHMAN'S PIPE *Aristolochia californica*

DESCRIPTION: A deciduous semi-woody vine to 12 ft. tall, twining and without tendrils, young stems slender, more or less pubescent; leaves alternate, ovate with a heart-shaped base, 1½-5 in. long, hairy on both sides, leaves appearing after the flowers; flowers borne singly or 2-3 on pendulous stalks from the previous season's wood, flowers pipe-shaped, greenish-purple, about 1 in. long, petals none, the flower formed of 3 united petal-like sepals; fruit capsule about 1-2 in. long containing numerous seeds.

FLOWERING: late January to April.

DISTRIBUTION: *Aristolochia californica* is found on low ground near streams in the low foothills of the middle and inner Coast Ranges from north of San Francisco Bay to the head of the Sacramento Valley and south in the foothills of the Sierra Nevada to Sacramento County. It is also occasionally found in Monterey County.

PROPAGATION: At the Rancho Santa Ana Botanic Garden the California Dutchman's Pipe has been propagated by digging rooted shoots from old plants during the dormant season. It is, however, reported that plants are easily grown from seed. This vine will grow in nearly any soil but it must have partial shade and an abundance of water as well as some support for the stems such as a tree or shrub over which it can grow.

USES: *Aristolochia californica* is of limited value as a shade producing vine. At the Botanic Garden it was successfully used for several years on the east side of a lath house where it was useful in cutting down the light in the lath house during the summer, and during the winter it was dormant and leafless thus allowing all the winter sunshine to enter. The species is, however, a most interesting native and well worth growing for its very curious flowers.

According to Rehder it was first introduced into cultivation in 1877.

PIPE-STEM CLEMATIS *Clematis lasiantha*

DESCRIPTION: A woody deciduous vine often climbing over shrubs and low trees for many feet, young branches hairy; leaves opposite, divided into 3 leaflets, leaflets roundish or elliptic-ovate, coarsely toothed and often more or less 3-lobed, 1-2 in. long; flowers borne singly on peduncles 2-6 in. long, flowers 1½-2½ in. across, white, either male or female the two borne on separate plants, petals absent but sepals petal-like, silky-hairy on the outside; achenes pubescent with long plumose tails 1 in. or more long when mature.

FLOWERING: April and May.

DISTRIBUTION: *Clematis lasiantha* is found in the Coast Ranges, Sierra Nevada and the mountains of southern California at altitudes of less than 2000 ft.

PROPAGATION: Propagation of this Clematis is by seeds which germinate readily when planted in flats in the fall. The young seedlings can be transplanted to individual pots later and they will then be ready to plant out either during the late spring or early fall depending upon how much care is to be given them.

In the garden they do best in a rather light soil with good drainage and, as in the case of nearly all species of Clematis, they should have their roots in the shade while the rest of the plant is in the sun. This can often be accomplished by placing them on the east or north side of a low wall or fence and then providing a trellis, shrub, or small tree for the plants to clamber over.

151

Clematis lasiantha fruit

Clematis lasiantha flowers

Uses: Since this species is not especially attractive when out of bloom it is probably best to allow it to climb over another plant and in this way the Clematis will not be noticed except when in flower. It should be pointed out, however, that if the vine is allowed to climb over a small or delicate shrub it will often kill it within a few years and therefore only coarse shrubs or trees should be used for this purpose.

If the plants are grown on a trellis they should be securely attached to the support to prevent the rather brittle stems from being broken by the winds.

Once established this species will grow without attention from the gardener although it will respond well to any care given it. While the young plants can not tolerate summer watering, especially if growing in heavy soil, older ones can be given small amounts with beneficial results.

Nothing is known about the horticultural history of this species. A native Clematis was used in a garden near Marysville as early as 1857 but it was probably *Clematis ligustici-folia,* a species native to the area, rather than *C. lasiantha.*

Lathyrus splendens

PRIDE OF CALIFORNIA   *Lathyrus splendens*

Description: A perennial climber as much as 8 ft. tall, stems slightly woody at the base; leaves alternate and divided into from 6-10 leaflets these distributed alternately on either side of the main axis of the leaf which terminates in from 1-3 tendrils, leaflets linear to elliptic-ovate, ⅝-1¼ in. long; flowers borne in axillary clusters 3-6 in. long with from

3-10 flowers, flowers wine-red or maroon, pea-shaped, about 2 in. long, the banner (upper petal of the flower) extremely deflexed (pointing backward in the opposite direction of the rest of the flower); fruit a flattened pod 3 in. long and ⅜ in. wide, seeds brown, about 3/16 in. in diameter, slightly flattened.

FLOWERING: March and April.

DISTRIBUTION: *Lathyrus splendens* is usually found in coarse decomposed granite in chaparral areas in San Diego County near the Mexican border and from there south into Baja California.

PROPAGATION: This plant is propagated by seeds which, for the best results, should be planted directly into 4-in. pots since the seedlings are somewhat difficult to transplant. Mirov suggests that the seeds be treated with hot water to hasten germination but at the Rancho Santa Ana Botanic Garden this has not been found necessary. Plantings may be made during fall or early spring and the young plants should be held over the first summer in the lath house and planted out the following fall. Pride of California (also known as Campo Pea) may be propagated from cuttings taken from new growth early in the spring. The cuttings root readily in sand but are difficult to transplant.

USES: Considerable thought must be given to where this species should be planted in the garden. The plants should have coarse well-drained soil with a little shade for the roots and something for them to climb over. A vigorous shrub is especially suitable although the plants can be trained onto a trellis or a fence. One rule which should be vigorously adhered to is that after the plants are established they should never be watered during the summer.

Lathyrus splendens has long been known to gardeners but it has never been common because of the difficulties encountered in handling the plants. It is, however, an extremely attractive vine when in flower and is well worth the effort required to grow it successfully. It was first discovered in 1882 and was grown at Kew in 1894 from seeds received from Dr. E. L. Greene.

DESERT GRAPE   *Vitis girdiana*

DESCRIPTION: A vigorous deciduous vine growing many feet long and becoming very woody at the base in old plants, young shoots and leaves densely hairy; leaves which are alternate and opposite the tendrils are broadly heart-shaped to ovate in outline, 2-5 in. broad, margins of leaf irregularly toothed and the entire leaf often distinctly lobed, lower surface of leaf densely hairy with long matted hairs; flowers borne in clusters opposite the leaves, flowers small, greenish, fragrant; berry black with a slight bloom, ⅛-¼ in. in diameter.

FLOWERING: May and June.

DISTRIBUTION: *Vitis girdiana* occurs along streams at elevations of less than 4000 ft. in the mountains of southern California, occasionally at the edge of the desert, north to Inyo County and south into Baja California. It is also found on Santa Catalina Island.

PROPAGATION: The Desert Grape may be grown from seeds sown in flats in the fall or by cuttings taken early in the spring. It is also possible to propagate this species by layering. The Desert Grape is not particular as to soil, even growing well in heavy adobe but it does require considerable water.

USES: This species is recommended as the best of the native vines for producing shade and is a most attractive plant for trellises or for planting along sunny walls, etc. The small fruits, while edible, are rather dry.

Vitis californica is in many ways similar to the Desert Grape. It differs mainly in having thinner leaves which are not as pubescent as are those of *V. girdiana* and the berries are purple with a dense bloom. It is found along streams from central California north into Oregon. Propagation and handling are the same as for the Desert Grape. *Vitis californica* has been in cultivation since 1890 according to Rehder.

6. Bulbs

California is rich in bulbous plants including such things as the Erythroniums, Fritillarias, Calochorti, and the lilies. Unfortunately many of these plants are difficult for the average gardener living in southern California to handle and therefore they must be left to the specialists. The following species however are rather easy to grow and can be recommended to anyone who will give them a little attention at least until they become established.

Brodiaea laxa

BRODIAEA   2½ feet   *Brodiaea laxa*

DESCRIPTION: Flowering stem slender, 1-2½ ft. tall from an usually deep-seated corm; leaves 2-3, basal and grass-like, usually about ⅔ as long as the stem; flowers borne in clusters of from 8 to nearly 50 at the tips of the stems, individual flower large, broadly funnelform in shape, 1¼-2 in. long, violet-purple in color.

DISTRIBUTION: *Brodiaea laxa* is found in adobe fields and on hillsides in the Coast Ranges from Oregon south to Los Angeles and San Bernardino counties and in the Sierra Nevada from Tehama County to Kern County. It is also found on San Clemente Island.

FLOWERING: March to May.

PROPAGATION: *Brodiaea laxa* may be propagated by seeds or by corms. Seed germinates readily but it takes several years to produce blooming size plants, so for practical purposes it is probably best to buy corms which will produce flowers the first season.

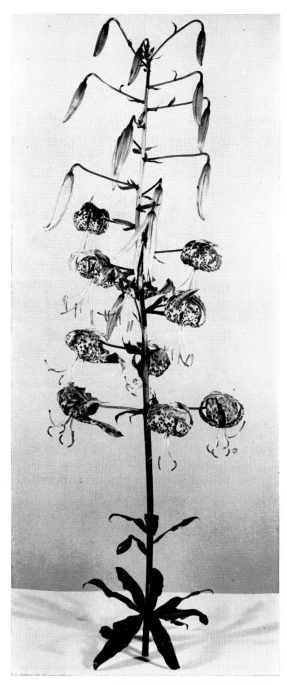

PHOTOGRAPH BY DOUGLAS EBERSOLE

Lilium humboldtii

This very beautiful species, which in its better forms reminds one somewhat of an Agapanthus, does well in the average garden where it should be given a deep, rather rich and gritty soil with light shade. Once established the plants should be left undisturbed.

According to the Royal Horticultural Society's Dictionary of Gardening, *Brodiaea laxa* was introduced into cultivation in 1832.

MARIPOLA LILY

MARIPOSA LILY   2½ feet   *Calochortus vestae*

DESCRIPTION: An herbaceous perennial from a corm, stem erect, as much as 2½ ft. tall, often branched; leaves linear, reduced upward; inflorescence 1-3-flowered, flowers erect, cup-shaped, up to 3 in. in diameter, composed of 6 creamy-white segments which may be flushed with lilac or rose, at the base of each segment there is a conspicuous velvet-brown hairy gland; fruit a linear erect 3-angled capsule.

DISTRIBUTION: *Calochortus vestae* is found in heavy clay soils in the North Coast Ranges from Humboldt County south to Napa and Sonoma counties.

FLOWERING: April to July.

Propagation of *Calochortus vestae* is either by seeds or corms. The seed, which may be sown in flats, germinates readily and the young seedlings may be allowed to complete one season's growth without transplanting. Extra care should be taken in watering the young plants since they are quite susceptible to damping-off. It is probably best to plant the one-year-old cormlets in specially prepared beds and allow them to remain there until they reach blooming size before planting them in their permanent location. It will usually require 3-4 years from the time the seed is planted until the plants bloom. For practical purposes it is probably best to buy full grown corms from dealers rather than to attempt to grow them from seed.

In the garden the plants should be given a fairly heavy but well-drained soil and they should have nearly full sun. The plants should have moderate amounts of water until they bloom, after which watering should be stopped. Probably more calochortus corms are lost because of rodents than from any other cause and it may be necessary to protect them by planting the bulbs in hardware-cloth baskets buried in the ground.

USES: *Calochortus vestae* is one of the largest and most attractive of the many native species of Calochortus, all of which are very beautiful but for the most part quite difficult to handle in most gardens. *C. vestae* is considered the easiest of the species to grow and once established they should be left undisturbed.

Calochortus vestae was introduced into cultivation in 1895.

HUMBOLDT LILY

HUMBOLDT LILY   6 feet   *Lilium humboldtii*

DESCRIPTION: An herbaceous perennial from a large scaly usually lop-sided bulb, scales as much as 2¾ in. long; stem stout, often 6 ft. or more tall (in the Botanic Garden they have reached 12 feet) and clothed with numerous shining oblong-lanceolate leaves up to 5 in. long and 1 in. broad, leaves arranged in whorls on the stem; flowers borne in a pyramidal-shaped inflorescence at the top of the flower-stalk, individual flower about 3 in. across, bright orange conspicuously dotted with maroon or purple spots, flower segments 6, about 2½-4 in. long, recurved forming a nodding turkscap blossom.

DISTRIBUTION: *Lilium humboldtii* occurs in the Sierra Nevada from Butte to Fresno County where it is found in rather dry heavy soil in the open woods below 4500 ft.

FLOWERING: June to August.

PROPAGATION: Propagation of the Humboldt Lily is either by seeds or by scales taken from the old bulbs. The seeds germinate readily when planted in flats and the young seedlings can be allowed to remain without transplanting for the first two seasons. The flats should be watered carefully to prevent damping-off and at the end of the growing season they should be gradually dried off and stored until the following spring. By the third year the bulbs should be large enough to plant in the garden. A few flowers may be expected that year but most of the plants will not bloom until the following season. This species can also be propagated by scaling old bulbs. This method is described in detail in Chapter IV.

In the garden the Humboldt Lily should be given a well-drained soil which contains considerable humus. It should also be given partial shade. Here at the Botanic Garden this species has done very well on partially shaded slopes under tall trees and shrubs. Once established, undisturbed plants will increase in size and vigor until they form specimens over 6 ft. tall and carrying up to 80 beautiful orange flowers.

Certainly the Humboldt Lily should be grown in every garden where conditions will permit since there are few finer or more spectacular native plants than this one when in flower. Woodcock and Stearn in their new book[1] call this lily the "glory of the Sierra Nevada Range."

Lilium humboldtii has long been in cultivation, being first discovered by Roezl in 1869 on the birthday of the noted German traveller and scientist, Baron F. H. Alexander von Humboldt after whom it was named.

Lilium humboldtii var. *ocellatum* has flowers which are a rich golden orange color with many maroon spots each surrounded by a crimson circle. This variety is found in the chaparral below 3000 ft. in Santa Barbara County south to the San Jacinto and Santa Ana Mts.

Lilium humboldtii var. *bloomerianum* is usually a smaller plant with leaves about half as wide as in the species and the flowers are not as richly colored as in the variety *ocellatum,* however, the spots are much the same as in that variety. This variety is found in the mountains in eastern San Diego County.

STAR ZYGADENE   *Zygadenus fremontii*

DESCRIPTION: An herbaceous perennial from a bulb which may be as much as 1¼ in. in diameter; leaves 3-4, long and narrow, somewhat fleshy, bright green, 8-18 in. long, stem 1-2¼ ft. tall bearing a few short leaves; flowers borne in a paniculate cluster containing many flowers, individual flowers fairly large, star-shaped, the six segments broadly oblong, acute at the tip, cream-yellow with a conspicuous greenish-yellow nectary near the base; capsule 1 in. long, oblong in shape, many-seeded.

DISTRIBUTION: *Zygadenus fremontii* is found in deep soil on brushy hillsides in the Coast Ranges south to southern California.

FLOWERING: February to June.

PROPAGATION: The Star Zygadene may be propagated either by seeds or bulbs. Seed sown in flats in the fall germinates in about a month and the seedlings can be allowed to make one season's growth without transplanting. The plants can be expected to bloom about the third year. This species is not especially particular as to soil and it will thrive in most situations.

USES: This very interesting native is recommended as a plant that starts blooming early in the spring and continues on for a considerable length of time.

---

[1] Hubert B. Drysdale Woodcock and William Thomas Stearn, *Lilies of the World,* 431 pp. Charles Scribner's Sons, 1950.

LITERATURE

Edmunds, L. L. *Native Plants for Ground Cover.* Jour. Calif. Hort. Soc. 4: 58-63, 1943.

———. *Pruning Ceanothus.* Jour. Calif. Hort. Soc. 8: 64-65, 1947.

———. *A Few California Shrubs.* Jour. Calif. Hort. Soc. 10: 143-147, 1949.

Everett, Percy C. *The California Penstemons.* El Aliso 2: 155-198, 1950.

McMinn, Howard E. *Sixteen Choice California Woody Plants Used in Landscaping.* Jour. Calif. Hort. Soc. 9: 70-74, 1948.

———. *Five Choice Native Shrubs for Landscaping Use.* Jour. Calif. Hort. Soc. 9: 178-183, 1948.

———. *Five More Native Shrubs.* Jour. Calif. Hort. Soc. 10: 17-22, 1949.

———. *Studies in the Genus Diplacus (Scrophulariaceae).* Madroño 11: 33-128, 1951.

Mirov, N. T. and Charles J. Kraebel. *Collecting and Handling Seeds of Wild Plants.* Civilian Conservation Corps Forestry Publication No. 5, 1939.

Mirov, N. T. *Additional Data on Collecting and Propagating the Seeds of Califorina Wild Plants.* Forest Research Notes No. 21, Calif. Forest and Range Exp. Sta., Berkeley, 1940, revised 1945.

Van Rensselaer, Maunsell, and Howard E. McMinn. *Ceanothus,* 308 pp., Santa Barbara Botanic Garden, Santa Barbara Calif., 1942.

United States Forest Service. *Woody-Plant Seed Manual,* United States Dept. of Agriculture Miscellaneous Publication No. 654, 1948.

INDEX

Entries in which there is a description of one of the 'recommended species' have the page numbers *italicized;* pages on which illustrations appear are in **bold face.**

INDEX

INDEX

163

INDEX

INDEX

INDEX